Eloquence

Writers
of
Ipswich
(Queensland, Australia)

I0689176

Contributors

Writers (alphabetically)
Joan Alexander
Carole Aveley
Philip J Bradbury
Jenny Chriswick
Judy de la Mare
Janet Findlay
Mark Grieveson
Paul Howlett
NK
Estelle McCrohan

Editing, text design, cover design and publishing by Philip J Bradbury ... with a huge number of great ideas, help, images and supplementary text - e.g. back-cover blurb - by all of the contributing writers in this book.

Printed by Ingram Sparks.
If you cannot find the book in your local book store you can find it online at:
www.philipjbradbury.com, or
www.ingramsparks.com

ISBN: 978-0-9954398-4-9

Foreword

I am rather honoured to be assembling a few words of wisdom, as a preface to introduce this publication.

In the literary world, my claim to fame is that I have been Chair of Ipswich Libraries since 2004. I also founded the fabulous *Ipswich Poetry Feast*, which is an annual national and international poetry competition. *The Feast* is in its 14th year and attracts over 1,000 entries each time we hoist up the flag.

This book, *Eloquence*, is independently published and is really interesting, colourful and varied. The book has provided a written venue for our very own Ipswich creative writers and promises to be the first of a continuing series.

These Wordsmiths are the unknown story tellers of Ipswich, Queensland, Australia. It is amazing what a summer writing school, via U3A, can roll out. These tales are from a special class of older writers who reflect on life experiences and local stories. Friendships were bonded between these pages and the eloquence of the writers is to be enjoyed.

I dips me lid to Philip J Bradbury and his group of wordsmiths.

Now, where did all those words come from!!!!!!

Cr David Pahlke, *Chair of Ipswich Libraries & Ipswich Poetry Feast*

Contents

Contributors	2
Foreword	3
How to look after a Rose	6
Instructions I	10
Chain Man Interruptus	12
A Darting Tourist	14
Party Dress	16
Snow White And The Seven Paper Hangers	17
My Favourite Dress	20
Old Friends	22
Instructions II	25
Underpants	26
Two Chickens	27
My Process To Becoming Politically Apathetic!	29
An Understandable Affectation	32
A Colourful Life	35
Another Siege	40
Instructions III	42
Chicken Kiev	44
Softly Spoken Words	46
A Walk in the Woods	49
The Yellow Satin Boxers	52
Westwood Towers	56
The Sacrifice Is Accepted	58
The Dirt Bike	61

Bella's Gift	62
H and G Pharmaceuticals	66
The Ant and the Grasshopper	69
The Emperor's New Clothes	72
Hansel and Gretel - A Fairy Tale	73
The Delivery	77
Knickers and Vicars	81
Wednesday's Child	83
Shooting Time	86
The Far Flung Pan	89
The Shrinking Dress	92
Chickens	94
The Game	96
The Magic Faraway Tree	100
Shorts	102
Chicken Soup	103
Give Me Time	104
Have You Never ...	107
The Impromptu Exercise	110
I Need Not Permission	113
Chooks, Bikes and Cars	115
The Old Woman Who Lived In A Shoe	118
Drinking Beer	120
Abbey Road Party	121
The Missing Links	124
Limericks	127
Biographies	*129*
Appendix	*132*

DO NOT READ
Under Penalty
of Law

How to look after a Rose

Janet Findlay

At the beginning, I usually go and sit on the old black vinyl chair with the split in the seat. The one located on the little ramp that leads up to the side door of The Cottage. Get myself as comfortable as possible while I'm waiting for Dan.

It's hard to predict exactly when he'll arrive. Sometimes he'll ring or text me with a curt message. *Twenty minutes* or *Won't be before 3* or *Mum hasn't woken up yet.* But I like to feel prepared. So, I either sit and breathe in the country air, close my eyes and practise relaxing, or play with my phone.

At some point, I'll see the red car heading up the driveway towards me. Past the first house, past the second, past the stables on the right. When Dan swings into the turning circle I get up, walk down the ramp, then greet him as he gets out of the driver's seat. Rose will be in the passenger seat either mumbling to herself with a pained expression on her fine-featured face, or else sitting stock still – staring ahead into nothing. Sometimes, she's there with her eyes closed, snoring.

I've given her a dart, so she should be okay, Dan might say as he opens the back door to get the striped cushion I use to support my back. Often on those occasions, I can see he looks tired. May well have been up all night watching out for his mother as she prowls restlessly through the house, or lies fully awake on her bed, jabbering.

Oh, that's good! I generally answer and grin at him. If she sleeps through the drive, that means it may not be necessary to constantly engage with her stream of utterances, but nothing is guaranteed here. Back at six? I might add as I get into the driver's seat and adjust it forward. Dan will likely as not, nod, and take off towards the stables, the wind ruffling his hair. There's something boyish in his stride still, even though he must be 50.

I take the car out of neutral, look across at Rose, maybe give her shoulder a pat if she's asleep. On the other occasions when she's awake and raving, I will greet her affectionately. Sometimes she responds to this. Then we head slowly down the long drive, with me being careful not to go too fast over the bumps and potholes. If I happen to hit one when she's conscious or semi-conscious, it's enough to elicit a loud, accusing Jesus Christ! And even though that's amusing for me, it must be alarming for her.

When I first started looking after Rose, the gate at the end of the drive would often be closed, so to have to locate and then fiddle with the remote control would delay our progress at an important juncture. For I quickly learned that the sooner I could swing the car out onto the New England highway and accelerate in steady increments up to a 100 k's, the better it was for my restless passenger. Rose prefers to be in constant motion.

Sometimes, when I stop at lights or at a crossing, she'll go C'mon, c'mon darling! and I have to tell her that I can't do that - if we both want to remain alive. Sometimes that'll prompt me to wonder if Rose does want to remain alive. But there's no way of knowing.

Generally, we take off for Warwick. I think Dan might once have thought his mother's carers would be content to drive round and round the suburbs or the centre of Toowoomba for 4 hours. Not me, not Rhonda, not her twin sister Irene. We may take different routes to Warwick but it's the same destination. I know Rhonda likes to drive off the highway, and explore all the winding unsealed roads, while Irene goes on the Highway there and back, twice in one afternoon. Me, I like to do both. Some stretches of main road, and then the little villages – Greenmount, Nobby, Clifton, Allora ... sometimes Leyburn, Karara ...

While we try in our various ways to make 4 hours of almost non-stop driving interesting for us, Rose, regardless of location, will either be staring, snoring or talking non-stop. Take me home darling, take me home, I want to go home darling...darling...are you there darling? Where are you? At this, she might swing round and look straight past me, sitting right next to her in the drivers' seat.

Here I am darling, I might reply, and I AM taking you home. I'm taking you home - the long way.

(Of course, 'home' can be a hard-to-define concept at the best of times. For Rose, it's definitely not the 70's brick bungalow connected to another brick bungalow that was occupied by the stable manager in the days when she and her husband used to breed racehorses. When she reaches THAT home, she still wants to go home.)

Back on the road to Warwick, although it may be exhausting for both driver and passenger to engage with this constant distraught theme, in some ways it's good when it happens in an intelligible language. At other times, Rose lapses into word substitutes. What were once words. Uttered in the same anguished tone, they mostly lose their consonants – and become a repetitive drone which may only vary in volume and intensity.

It can be a brief respite then to stop in the pretty town of Allora, for a coffee, juice or toilet break. In whatever state of consciousness my dear friend is in, I will always explain to her what I'm about to do and that I'll be as quick as possible about it. She can still surprise me by saying quite sensibly, Yes darling. Parking as close as possible to the required facility, I'll carefully lock the doors, accomplish my endeavour and return to the car.

We may share a coffee or a water – ye plee darling – and that is the moment I feel she is most present, and almost content. If you take advantage of that though, if you linger too long, it'll soon be C'mon, c'mon darling! And I do respond straightaway (though I may need to readjust the mirror or retune the sound system which has been mysteriously altered in my absence). So we head off, on the road again, almost at Warwick.

Driving along the back road from Allora to Warwick, takes about 20 minutes. It's a winding road in parts, and you often encounter young men in utes impatient to overtake you. For I like to slow down a bit on this part of the journey, take in the spectacle of distant, deep indigo mountains hit by golden sunlight, or in the summer, marvel at an endless field of sunflowers, or an expanse of soft purple flowers carpeting the foreground of a white country church. At these times, to me, it's like travelling through a painting.

When we reach Warwick, if I haven't managed to get a coffee

earlier, I'll head to the McDonalds drive-through, past the over-sized churches and the straight, rose-lined streets. Either way, we're never there for that long.

I usually put on the same Mozart CD on the way back. It goes with the scenery. I know every track by heart now. We all do. As Dan says, you never get sick of good music. And sometimes, I like to think it gets through to Rose a little…

Darling, darling…. Are you there darling? Where are you?

I'm here darling. And I'm at home. At home in the beauty of the landscape, at home in this music, at home with you in the Darling, Darling Downs….

C'mon darling. C'mon. Let's go!

Instructions I

Carole Aveley

First visualize the shape you want to create: sketch the outline that pleases you most - hour glass? Venus de Milo? Decide on size - especially height, think about where it will be situated; maybe half a meter, or one meter or even taller; make sure the curves are generous.

Select a suitable piece of wood, in my case I chose a log about six centimetres in diameter; cut it to the required length, mine was approximately thirty centimetres. Secure it in the lathe at both ends. Take a one cm chisel and shape the top end, rounding it to a suitable size to provide a substantial holder for a fitting; shape the other end to match, but make it slightly larger than the top in order to keep the proportions balanced. This will give your figure a good shape to build from

The main central section should now be shaped starting just below the holder, carefully form a slender neck, flowing to the shoulders, then gracefully and smoothly downward to the waist expanding in a generous curve to rounded hips which must fit smoothly onto the base, much like the ample curves of a Venus de Milo.

Before you remove it from the lathe, you must fashion a one centimetre protrusion from the centre below the base. You may then cut through the log at the base of the protrusion. Release this end and remove the whole item from the lathe. Place the item firmly in a vice and using a chisel square off your protrusion. This will be used to secure your finished product to its stand.

Next you must select a larger cut of wood to form the stand, about nine centimetres in diameter by three centimetres deep suits the proportions of my item. Place it in the lathe, and shape it to balance the length of the main structure. Remember the taller the item the larger the base stand to prevent it being top heavy. Getting the size right is vital or your final item will not stand firmly.

Remove from lathe, secure in the vice and using a wide chisel cut out a square in the centre to exactly match the protrusion in your main item. Test for size until you are sure the male and female parts fit snugly together. Now glue them together.

You are now ready to varnish your item. Leave to dry overnight. Your item is now almost complete. Using the lathe you must carefully drill through from base to top in one operation.

Cut a three meter length of electrical flex and thread up from base to top. Now attach a brass holder for an electric globe and connect up your flex. Lastly insert a switch into the flex about ten centimetres away from the base stand and attach a plug onto the end to connect to the electrical supply.

Stand back, admire and wait for the compliments to pour in!!!

Answer: See Appendix on page 132

Chain Man Interruptus

Mark Grieveson

Forty four years ago I worked for around eighteen months as a chain-man for a local authority. Now this has nothing to do with a chain gang although I suspect many chain-men would have qualified as members if we had had them here.

For interest sake I looked up "chain-man" in the internet Urban Dictionary and found the following definition quote: "a shabby-arsed useless tit of an assistant who attempts to follow orders given to him by a Land Surveyor." It appears that little has changed in four decades.

In the next entry it defined career chain-men as "nasty rabid, fly blown and flea bitten pieces of work who, for some reason, are all smokers and have filthy beards."

It would seem I still qualify on at least one of those criteria.

You may gather from this that chain men are rather a rough and ready bunch and, in the main, you'd be spot on.

But as I've often found to my relief, even in the most unlikely places, there lurks at least one outsider - outsiders being people who do not subscribe to mainstream sensibilities. In fact they generally hold them in contempt, believing they are shackles to personal growth.

There were two other such creatures in my gang - both autodidacts like myself for whom reading was an essential drug.

One of them Joe (name changed to protect the guilty) and I had endless conversations about Sartre and Camus and Hesse and Rilke. I first read Lord of the Rings by borrowing his copy. I recall that he gave me a copy of Sartre's Nausea for my 19th birthday. Perhaps typically, a closer examination of the book suggested it had been stolen from a public library.

The other outsider was of a quite different species. David was a devotee of Timothy Leary whose book The Politics of Ecstasy was one of the bibles of hippiedom. It famously advocated "Turn on, tune in, drop out". David was a connoisseur of inner space. He rolled me my first joint and supplied my only (to date) LSD tab.

But back to the main chase … quite often we chainmen were required to cut a line, that is, remove all impediments to providing the surveyor a direct line of sight on a particular bearing . In scrub land this was done using brush hooks and axes. Chainsaws were available but it was considered sissy to use one except in unavoidable circumstances. Axemanship was a highly prized art and one which I never mastered.

One morning three of us chainmen were working on the Ipswich bank of the Brisbane River below the Colleges Crossing Bridge. This area was far more remote and bushy than it is today. The required line of sight had been determined the previous day and the foliage to be removed daubed with red paint. The topography was undulating due to thousands of years of floods sweeping across the landscape.

The old hand in charge was a rough nut who answered only to "Boss". Nobody allegedly knew his real name. His talk, unlike Nixon's tapes which had recently become public, was expletive never deleted. In fact I learned to swear without blushing from him as he considered it a prerequisite to be a member of his gang.

We made good progress for several hours following a 6.30 am start and were well out of sight of the road by the time we stopped for smoko. We rested from our exertions almost too tired to talk. Only an occasional bird call and the distant shushing of the Brisbane River could be heard. Boss suddenly whispered that he could hear someone close by. Then we all could hear the suggestive noise. We got up and quietly moved in its direction.

We edged the rim of a major depression and there, in front of us, was a naked young couple going hell bent for leather as the saying goes. They were completely oblivious of our presence.

I was totally embarrassed for the couples' sake. Not so Boss who was made of sterner stuff. He yelled out "Can I go seconds?"

Sudden coitus interruptus resulted.

A Darting Tourist

Estelle McCrohan

A lizard – or he hoped it was only a lizard – slid over his ankle as he hunkered down on his stomach in the lush tropical bush. He didn't dare move. Only his eyes widened as he gazed at the track ahead.

He knew he was well hidden and his camouflage outfit helped make him invisible. He drew in his breath as the faint sounds of his quarry's footfalls sounded. Just as he had expected and planned for. Now imminent action had him tensed and ready.

He felt the weapon in his hands, the trigger beneath his finger. He had trained for this particular assignment for hours – days even. He drew in his breath and tensed. The footfalls were much clearer, each sounding louder than the last.

It was time!

His target was almost fully in sight – now!

Rising to his full height he aimed and –

"Hey! You there! What do you think you're doing? Stop!"

His finger on the trigger tightened, but the sudden eruption of a tourist from the opposite side of the track caused him to turn slightly and the target halted, watching as the tourist stood transfixed, staring, silent. The cause was only too evident.

"O Lordy! Where did you come from mate?"

He sprang from his secure hide and rushed across to the fallen man.

Glancing at the intended target, his embarrassment was enhanced by the con-descending look from the cassowary, as if to say 'so much for YOU, miserable sod. As if you could pin ME down with your silly dart gun.'

How was he going to explain to the wounded tourist when he came to, he wondered as the bird wandered off into the undergrowth. Unhurried and unstudied.

And how to explain the failure of this expensive exercise to the scientists at the zoo?

Party Dress

Janet Findlay

I've got a party dress
That I keep for best
So I wear it less
Than anything else

It's got splashes of colour
Like Kandinsky's art
Some shapes are vivid
Others are dark
It's got shoulder pads
That come from the Ark
And a skirt that turns
In a circle

It hangs from my wall
In free fall
Still but full
Of music

Snow White And The Seven Paper Hangers

Philip J Bradbury

Once upon a merrie olde thyme, back before cycle helmets, pool fences and shopping hours were invented to protect us from ourselves, there lived a woodcutter's daughter. She was born very early in her life and, about that time, decided that work was for others and she would simply enjoy herself. Accordingly, she was called Gretel which means *Lazy One*. Her diligent, gullible brother was called Hansel. This meant *Stupid Oaf* in Gretellian.

Gretel could never understand her dopey father who was up and down his whole life – he cut trees down and then cut them up. He never got beyond the poverty line, continually had blisters and his wives always left him in disgust. Gretel determined that she would have the opposite – a life of never-ending riches, nice hands and constant, obedient men.

To this end she practised her devious arts on Hansel. One time, when her father and his latest wife were out cutting things down and up, Gretel thought she'd get Hansel to steal lollies from the lolly shop up the path in the woods. It was, in fact, a rather magical lolly shop for the whole building was made of lollies and the sweet old lady who owned it kept renovating and extending it.

Gretel told Hansel the sweet lady was, in fact, a bad witch and needed to get her comeuppance and he was just the man to do it. Hansel bristled with indignant pride at this – as any stupid oaf would do – and awaited his orders. He loped off with the map she'd drawn and followed him at a discrete distance to witness the fun. Unfortunately, he got his lefts and rights back to front and they were soon hopelessly lost.

Luckily, the wily old wolf soon appeared. Gretel told Hansel to hide while she drew her shawl around her and pretended she was a wizened old lady, hardly worth eating. She wangled the lolly shop directions out of him and then she gave Hansel the secret signal. He rushed out and chopped the wolf's head off. She later blamed her father for that.

They eventually found the old lady's shop and, by now, Hansel's dander was well and truly up and his common sense was out to lunch. He rushed into the shop – meaning to grab the old lady and give her a large piece of his tiny mind – tripped on the step and fell into the cauldron of peppermint jaffas she was brewing. The lady's kind husband, a medic at the Snow Queen's palace, scooped Hansel out, gave him mouth-to-mouth resuscitation and salved his burns. Hansel did recover but, from that time, resembled a golf ball with jaffa dents all over his body. He also smelled of peppermint all the time and had a hard time fending off female admirers … not that he tried very hard.

Of course, Gretel thought this was hilarious, even after she was charged as an accessory to attempted murder. Hansel was let off out of sympathy and Gretel was let out on bail. Her father was furious when he eventually found his errant children. He grounded them both for a month; a punishment Gretel deemed way too harsh for a simple bit of fun. She then managed to entice a local char girl – the one with the three ugly sisters – to dress up as Gretel, mope about the house doing menial jobs while Gretel went off in search of fun and other menials.

At the local pub she met up with some interesting chaps with black shirts, white ties, white shoes and with Italian sounding names. They induced her to try some of their nice white powder. It was very expensive, apparently, and she was ecstatic with the effect it had on her. She ordered a container load, convincing them her father was Old King Cole, son of the Black Prince, and he'd pay up tomorrow. She became quite fond of this white powder and soon earned the nickname of Snow White.

It was about this time that she met a group of wallpaper hangers who were unemployed on account of their diminished height. They could only wallpaper small houses and small-house people had no money for wallpaper.

When the Italian chaps caught up with her father, demanding payment and making offers he couldn't refuse, he was enraged. He set off through the forest in his seven league boots, stomping and slashing everything in sight. He never found her but kept stomping and slashing and eventually created the desert-wasted land of Australia.

Meanwhile, Gretel tripped off to live with the seven short wallpaperers, giving them a daily dose of white powder and had them slaving for her night and day and everyone lived stoned ever after.

My Favourite Dress

NK

My favourite dress is dead
Worn out by time and washing
We've been through a lot together
My favourite dress and I

We've been through thick
and thinner
(I'm talking about my waist)
We've been out to work
And to dinner
My favourite dress and I

5 times I've tried to divorce it
I've put it in the bin
The edges are frayed
The seams given way
The material's awfully thin

But I just can't manage to do it
I love that dress so much
It makes me happy to wear it
And throw it out?
Too much!

So my dress and I go gardening now
No high heels and make up for us
We get dirty and wet
We wear gumboots and sweat
 My beautiful dress and I.

So we're still having fun together
My beautiful dress and I
Out now in the fine sunny weather
Instead of at dinner or work
One day it'll fall right off me
And my friends and my neighbours will smirk

Thank goodness that dress is dead they'll say
We thought it would never die
But I'll mourn us
And miss us
My favourite dress and I

Old Friends

Joan Alexander

They met every six months. This arrangement had been ongoing for the last ten years. The four women had worked together for most of their working life, and when retirement had been welcomed, they had decided upon this regular meeting. An understanding city hotel had allowed them to sit for hours over coffee and sandwiches, as long as it was on one of the less busy days. In return the friends had praised the hotel to many subsequent customers.

Today was the meeting day and Beth was looking forward to seeing the other three. She dressed with care. She had lots to tell her friends of a recent holiday that she and her husband had enjoyed in Scotland. She drove her car to the station car park and caught the train into the city. When Beth arrived at the hotel she found her three friends were already there and were seated at a discreet corner table. With their usual affectionate greeting, it was obvious they were delighted to be in each other's company again.

Barbara, Margaret and Helen told of their previous six months, which had mainly consisted of the usual family affairs, all thankfully of the pleasant variety which included the birth of a baby before the next get together. The friends knew each other's families well and were most interested. They turned towards Beth and asked her of her exciting holiday.

Beth described arriving in Edinburgh in time for the Festival and of the enjoyment of the half a dozen performances they had seen. Also of walking the streets that had been described in some recent novels by Alexander McCall Smith. The main purpose of their visit, however was to explore over seven days the Inner and Outer Hebridean Islands. They had travelled to Glasgow and were collected the next morning by a small bus with the other ten travellers, to travel to Oban driving the length of beautiful Loch Lomond. After a lunch at Oban, they travelled by ferry along the Sound of Mull to Craigmure. Then a bus to the loveliest small township named Tobermory. The houses lining the quay were all painted in different colours and were so picturesque. The group was booked in to a large old hotel built of stone and were grateful for the comfortable four-poster beds. The views were lovely. That evening the travellers met together socially for dinner. At this stage Beth became somewhat breathless as she described that evening.

"We were sitting with three others, an elderly man and his wife and a much younger woman whom I took to be their daughter. They were extremely pleasant and told of some of their recent trips, which included a walking tour. As we had recently walked through some Swiss villages I mentioned how we had so enjoyed the beauty of the mountains. I don't know how that comment lead to talking about mountain climbing ... but it did! I then spoke of climbing some mountains near to where we lived. At this stage my husband quite obviously changed the subject, he evidently couldn't reach far enough under the table to kick me, but I got the message that I should shut up. Later that night in our room, I asked why he had stopped me talking. He then told me we had been dining with Sir John Hunt and his wife. When I still looked puzzled he explained that Sir John had been the leader of the successful conquest of Mt. Everest in 1953 by Sir Edmund Hilary and Sherpa Tenzing Norgay. Oh My Goodness, I felt so stupid!"

As Beth completed her story, her friends realised that she still felt dismayed at what she considered her foolish attempt at dinner conversation with such distinguished persons. They tumbled over each other to reassure Beth that none of the others at the table would have even remembered the conversation. They encouraged her to tell them of the rest of the Hebridean adventure.

Beth sketched in a few of the highlights that followed that night in Tobermory, a visit to Fingal's Cave, near Staffa , the Island of Iona, and all the while travelling over the beautiful shiny, silvery grey waters of the lochs and the more open waters towards the Outer Hebrides. They had travelled by bus down the islands of Lewis and Harris, finishing up in Barra where the ferry would take everyone back to Oban.

As they departed, Beth decided to remain on the top deck of the ferry so as to remember every last detail of the fascinating island and the sparkling silvery-grey waters. She thought she was alone as it was a cold afternoon and most passengers had stayed in the warm interior. Suddenly in one corner of the deck she noticed a young woman with her elbows on the railing and holding a handkerchief to her face. She was dabbing at tears running down her face. She looked so distressed that Beth approached her and gently asked her what the matter was. The girl said that it was just because of leaving. She loved the islands so much and had been spending her summer holidays there for some years, and each time leaving affected her as if departing from a beloved friend. Beth was glad the reason was not as dire as she had anticipated, but as the girl was so distressed Beth remained with her and as they chatted the lass regained her composure and sometime later they returned to the ferry's sitting room and farewelled each other.

At last they reached Oban and general farewells were made as all were heading in different directions.

Beth continued her story. "We said goodbye to the Hunts and wished them a safe return to their home. Mrs Hunt kissed us both, me first, and then as my husband hesitated Mrs Hunt leaned into him and kissed him on the cheek also. My husband responded by saying to her, 'that's the first time I've been kissed by a lady.' I just muttered under my breath, thanks a lot!"

The friends all laughed at that conclusion, and asked Beth if she felt better having told them the story. She said she did, and now understood the saying that confession was good for the soul. They shared one last coffee and made a date for their next meeting.

Instructions II

Estelle McCrohan

Head first is the best approach. Just make sure you are secure in your position, able to relate and adjust to sudden undulations and changes of attitude.

Your fingers should not be too slick. The slot itself should be lubricated sufficiently. As you lower the item in, make sure it is a perfect fit – not too slack. Even a little tight will be good.

The screw should be perfected when the implement adjusts naturally and you are able to withdraw slowly without ill effect. Ensure that you yourself maintain perfect equilibrium when the natural state is attained.

Before leaving, ensure all is in good working order and you are heading in the right direction. If not, further adjustments may be necessary but a delicate touch is required while making sure all parts are in their natural and optimum order.

Should any further adjustments be required it is imperative that the slot is not over-worked by the item becoming bent or skewed, and has not become dry or overly tight.

All should now be well – your journey will be pleasant and full of friendly accord.

Answer: See Appendix on page 132

Underpants

Judy de la Mare

Large loose ones are known as bloomers,
Queen Vic wore them, there are rumours.
In the States they are the panty,
And material wise, very scanty.
For English girls it is the knicker,
Small or large you be the picker.
Here downunder the undies trade,
Many different sorts are made.
Small and stylish is the brief,
Neatly fitting gives relief.
Or the hipster lying low,
Under jeans it is the go.
Some girls prefer a little zing,
For them the g-string is the thing.
Our sporty types are after shorts,
They firm and hold to all reports.
So ladies have a choice of lots,
Solid colours or polka dots.
Happy buns are what we need,
And no vpl[1] is our creed.

---

1   vpl = visible panty-line

Two Chickens

Judy de la Mare

Chickens crowded in a cage – such a sad sight to see these poor battery hens crammed almost on top of one another, struggling to be free, whilst covering themselves in shit. Sad little faces, open beaks and the eyes reflecting each other's terror. In nature there is a pecking order but these poor animals know only disorder and then death.

I have arrived to save just two – all I can take home with me. Who do I choose – and in making my choice leave the others to suffer their terrible fate.

Tears fill my eyes and I almost blindly pick a little brown hen and then a speckled girl with a twisted leg, a misshapen beak and almost no feathers. They are stuffed into a cardboard box and I take them home.

There is an old aviary at my place and as I gently take them out of the box I give them names. Little brown hen is Matilda and speckled girl is Maggie. I name her after Bob Dylan's "Maggie's Farm". The aviary must be a palace to them, with plenty of room to walk around, clean water and lots to eat, but for the first few days they hardly move, making weak chirps and huddling together. Slowly with gentle coaxing and fresh grubs they take an interest in life and settle in. Matilda lays an egg accompanied by a lot of chicken talk but poor little Maggie who has trouble walking, has not produced. As she can't venture far afield I start taking her with me into the garden. As I weed and dig the soil she sits beside me looking on. Then I begin talking to her – firstly about the chores that I need to do, and then about the weather.

Weeks go by and she is putting on weight and her feathers have grown back. Both Matilda and Maggie appear to be happy hens now. Matilda is giving me five eggs each week and Maggie gives me company in the garden. I have moved on to discussing more serious subjects with her – cooking, fashion and television dramas. As I talk she utters quiet little chicken clucks as if she is in agreement with me. When I take her back to Matilda I hear them discussing chicken matters together.

The weather suddenly turns cold and wet and for several weeks I remain indoors and our outings are put on hold. On the first fine day I can't wait to get outside again and Maggie seems equally pleased. She appears to have missed our talk sessions and before I start speaking she gets in first. Maggie must have been doing a lot of thinking during the weeks inside and now all those thoughts came tumbling out of her mouth.

From the sounds she made, I decided that she was philosophizing on life – how was it that she and Matilda were the chosen ones while the rest ended up as dog food. Her bright little eyes told so much and while I searched for fat witchetty grubs as a special treat, it was with her misshapen beak that she spoke with such eloquence.

My Process To Becoming Politically Apathetic!

Mark Grieveson

These days I try not to debate political issues which, like religious ones, generally eschew rationality and rely overwhelmingly on personal emotional responses.

But this was not always the case. In my more radical youth, I participated in street marches and would debate politics until the cows came home.

My disaffection was a gradual process, a death by the proverbial thousand cuts.

There used to be politicians who one could look up to – and I don't mean height, although both Whitlam and Fraser were six foot four inches. But there were people on both sides who were inspirational and unafraid to speak their minds on all issues, as compared with the many small minded party apparatchiks of today. I fondly remember the repartee between Jim Killen (Liberal) and Jim Daly (Labour) on opposite sides but great friends all the same.

Whitlam was the greatest inspiration in my experience – a veritable colossus with a well-stocked mind, a genuine lover of the arts and a mordant off the cuff wit. He offered promise, a positive vision buttressed by genuine policy.

I'll always remember his reply to a persistent heckler wanting to know his opinion on abortion: "Let me make quite clear that I am for abortion and, in your case Sir, we should make it retrospective." He was invited to give the eulogy at Killen's funeral: the only better one I've heard is Noel Pearson's at Whitlam's own funeral in 2014.

But today where are the visionaries to uplift our national spirit, inspire our young to right our wrongs, to lead us into the promised land? "Jobs and growth" and "they will take Medicare away" just don't cut it in the inspiration stakes and this lack of vision contributes mightily to our national apathy.

Both sides now tend to overblame their opponents past actions for current political woes. I suspect the only Prime Minister who didn't do this was Edmund Barton, Australia's first Prime Minister! But as mature people do in life, why can't political parties simply say, "We got it wrong, we miscalculated and will attempt to do it properly next time"

In recent times I noticed a disturbing tendency for politicians to openly exaggerate the actions they intend to take to or the actions they infer their opponents will do. It hid under the rubric of 'non-core promises' following inaction after a previous election. As if a change of name could somehow mollify the seriousness of what it really is – lying

I've given up real hope that any change of government will bring meaningful change. They simply appear afraid to take necessary action that might be unpopular, like raising taxes (not necessarily income tax) to repair the budget rather than hurting the less well off.

I can understand people who feel disempowered or disenfranchised and lodge a protest by voting for fringe parties like say the fictional One Neuron Party (any resemblance to a real party is purely coincidental). I believe that crucial issues like climate change, housing affordability, detention centres, hidden corporate interests in government, marriage equality, job losses and, more recently, Centrelink overpayment letters and politician expenses require courage, innovation and wisdom.

In fact, it needs a revolution in thinking and ethics of the type that only widespread public support can spark. Maintain the Rage, Occupy Wall Street, the Save Our Sons movement during the Vietnam War … where has our once buoyant impulse for genuine and fair reform gone.

I think the incipient progressive movement requires an anthem and I humbly suggest the following as a first draft ...

You put the left party in
And they throw the money about
So you do the hokey pokey
And you turn around
That's what it's all about

So you put the right party in
And they penalize the poor
So you do the hokey pokey
And you turn around
That's what it's all about

You put your head in
You put your head out
You bang it hard against the wall
And vow to vote "none of the above"
Until the bastards grow up.

An Understandable Affectation

Mark Grieveson

He came into the world the usual way, as the song says, completely unaware of his change in accommodation.

His first sustained inkling of separateness involved sun, sand, sea and a dead fish. He was walking small hand in big along a beach when a very still creature loomed large in his world. A thing with a mesmerizing ancient mariner eye that called out to be gingerly touched, then pushed and finally poked hard enough to discharge its watery contents.

Thereupon images from subsequent days, weeks and months came thick and fast like some psychic kaleidoscope. Some stayed fixed on the photographic plate of his mind while others danced away like dew at dawn, possibly to return in future dreams.

A momentous encounter with a large hissing goanna was remembered because of a sensed threat of danger. As was the experience of relief when his mother's hand jerked him back to safety.

His body and awareness grew within the safe cocoon of family. There was always his father and more particularly his mother to kiss better his hurts and defang the unknown.

Home was a shack backed by bush and serenaded by a kookaburra sunrise. His father rode off each morning on an ancient bicycle, trousers held in place by fascinating metal clips. And, on the weekend, his dad took him for rides on the same venerable machine. They often went to the bake house to buy half a loaf of freshly baked bread wrapped in soft paper. And on the return, he enjoyed feasting on its sweet innards. In response to this pretend offence, his mother would make him a vegemite sandwich with a hole in the middle, a secret game just between them.

And then out of seeming nowhere, catastrophe – his mother fell ill, deathly ill, and was to be hospitalized for an indefinite period. He couldn't fathom what this meant or how or even if it would change his day to day life. And when he was told he would have to stay in a place with other children, well, what did that involve? His perception of time was limited to the possibility of a next day. He was four and a half years old.

Thus began some hard times:

Being woken up early … fed on lumpy porridge at breakfast instead of corn flakes … the use of boiled cabbage as the main vegetable (the very memory acts as an emetic) … and worse, the lack of his beloved tomato sauce to make the meals more palatable .

But the hardest to endure by far was the reign of terror after dark. There was a large boy, Reynolds by name (he would never forget that name), whose specialties were jumping onto sleeping smaller boys or whispering foul names using unfamiliar but obviously taboo words. Fear prevented any attempt at reporting the offence.

But there were also many good memories:

Children marching hand in hand to the nearby beach. He always recalled the bonfire and sky rockets on Guy Fawkes night and the faint hiss as the expended missile landed in the water.

Communal singing around the piano with This Old Man, He Played One being the never tired of favourite.

Listening to the radio en masse before bed (Greenbottle was mandatory – children echoed the drawn out Goo...od Morning Sir with absolute delight)

Playing with other children in the tree lined grounds and a large skipping rope with lines of children trying to enter and exit without tripping up.

Looking at the pictures in the meagre collection of Boys and Girls Own Annuals in the library.

And the remembered small kindnesses of some of the overworked staff.

The months advanced. There were looked for weekly visits from his father and often a grandparent or two. He commenced school from the home and remembered sitting in a hot room reciting the times tables. He learnt to read quickly and discovered the ecstasy of escaping the world via a book – an addictive experience that held good in later years. He discovered that words were better than pictures as purveyors of the wonders of the world at large. And some stories were so exciting that he felt compelled to continue to read them under the bed covers with a purloined torch.

Reynolds had left the place at Christmas and had no obvious successor as torturer at large, thereby evoking a general sense of relief.

And then on one visit there was his mother – thinner, greyer and less vital. And her magic words "We've come to take you home".

And as the car turned out of the entrance, he looked back and, in much later years, he liked to say he believed he saw an angel with a whirling fiery sword standing at the gate to prevent a return.

An understandable affectation.

A Colourful Life

Janet Findlay

The Princess – as she was called – lived on the second floor of an old block of flats opposite a railway station. On almost any day, of any season, she could be found holding court in her tiny, cramped lounge room, entertaining a guest or two, with tales of a glorious and, it must be said, questionable past.

If you happened to be there when the afternoon freight train thundered by, likely as not you would send the fragrant Earl Grey in your bone china teacup flying, momentarily baptising the surprised cat, or worse still, scalding yourself in the lap.

Unfazed by the train, the Princess might rise from her recliner and continue her anecdote from the kitchenette, raising her voice to an appropriate pitch, before returning with a sponge and bucket which she would place, like an offering, at your feet.

The first time this happened to me, it took a minute to realise this was to make my own repairs, to mop up the spreading stain on my skirt or possibly to dab the cat.

And all the while Theodora, for that was her name, would continue to talk, and all the while I would continue to listen. For the Princess had had at least nine lives. And at least eight of them sounded fascinating.

"Of course, things were going swimmingly for me darling, when I lived with Pepe the fraudulent art dealer! Parties on the yacht that lasted for days! I was pals with pollies and undercover police … oh, and the artists! Did I ever tell you darling, about the time on the harbour when I wrote some haiku on Brett Whiteley's torso? It was just as a storm coming up, the boat began to pitch and dive and my pen went beserk! Brett of course, was out to it – he'd flaked below deck - but my 17 syllables scrawled wildly on his scrawny bod in the middle of a cyclone, became immortalised that day! Not just because I'd mistakenly used the permanent marker, but because he loved it when he came to! Yes, darling, Brett loved it so much that he reproduced it in a painting that his ex-wife later sold for squillions …. the bitch … and it was my design!"

At this point in the story, or one of many like it, the Princess might get her faraway look, stroll across to a small ever-open window, carefully place a satin-tipped cigarette into a holder and turn back at look at you – through a cloud of smoke – as though she was wondering how on earth you ended up there. Even, Alastair the cat, sensing a change in mood, might yawn insolently, stretch out and parade his cream and ginger beauty before you – as if adding insult to injury.

Some of our mutual friends thought me mad to visit the Princess at that time of day, risking the consequences of the afternoon express train. But it was the best time for me, having other obligations in the morning and evening, and generally, it was worth risking a few splashes of hot tea. For in this dull town, she was larger than life and gave me access to adventures I wouldn't have been game enough to embark on myself.

"I'm having trouble sleeping Abigail," she said to me one time when the weather was beginning to change, and the few trees that stood between the flats and the station were shedding their leaves.

"I'm not surprised," I said. "If I heard that jolly announcement, Please stand behind the yellow safety line, fifteen times a day – I'd never be able to relax either!"

Theodora laughed. "Oh darling, that's water off a duck's back to me now. No, it's just that I can't seem to get comfortable no matter how hard I try. I've experimented with three different mattresses. I even got Barry from downstairs to adjust the legs of my bed to – well, you know the slope of the fl –"

We both heard the thundering of the approaching train. I laid down my cup on an adjoining table and firmly placed my hand over the top. She drummed her fingers idly on the arm of her Lazy boy – this time waiting for the train to pass rather than competing with it. When its final shuddering had eased, and the pictures on the wall had settled back into place, she calmly picked up where she'd left off. "To the slope of the floor."

"And did that help?" I returned the cup to my lips. The Earl Grey always tasted better after the train had passed through.

"No, not in the least!" The Princess was frowning.

I could see she was tired. The lines on her face were etched in deeply. Her faded blonde hair, once such a source of pride to her, hung in wispy strands, escaping the thin knot she wound it into. "I really don't know what to do."

She looked at me appealingly, and for the first time she seemed to me vulnerable.

"Perhaps you're stressed about something," I suggested. Then I quickly took a gulp of my tea. I had an idea you didn't suggest that the Princess experienced stress. I was right.

"Stress, hah!" she laughed a little harshly and her dark eyes fired up then. "Darling, I don't get stress – I give it!"

It was an old line. One she'd used several times before in the telling of different stories about husbands, lovers, employers, telephone companies. I laughed along with her and she seemed to pick up then, moving to another topic completely.

"Now, when are you going on holiday Abbey? You have to get that mother of yours put into respite care for a while or you'll be the one getting stressed!"

Touche.

I did eventually go on holiday. Not far, just up to the Coast. It was wonderful to walk along the beach in a Queensland winter and soak up all the enlivening effects of the ocean. When I came back, I didn't feel like picking up the strands of my old routine straightaway, so it was some months before I saw Theodora again.

When I did finally knock on the screen door of her flat, I was shocked by the figure that crept down the narrow passage to let me in. The usual proud bearing was gone. The Princess was stooped and thin.

"Princess!" I exclaimed. "Are you okay?" I bent to give her a hug. Her body felt frail and birdlike.

"No darling, I'm feeling dreadful. I've virtually not slept since I saw you last. I've tried every possible configuration of mattress, but it's just I can't get comfortable whatever I do!"

Instead of graciously leading me into her lounge room as she usually did, I lead her. I settled her into the lazy boy and took my customary place on the couch. I glanced at the clock on the bookshelf. It was 3.10.

The Princess caught my look. She gave a sudden snort of laughter. "Why don't you make us a cup of tea Abigail? It's almost time for the train!"

I wasn't sure whether I was being sent up or not. But I laughed weakly and obligingly went into the kitchenette to do the honours. Theodora issued instructions from her chair. "We'll have the floral cups. You know where the sugar is don't you? Use the milk with the blue top! Oh, hurry up, here's the train!"

At that point, the Princess began to laugh. But it was a laugh that grew wild and escalated into a breathless, gasping bark. The cat looked alarmed and crouched as if to spring. The train hurtled its way along the tracks as I lurched back into the room with a loaded tray. The cat sprang. I side-stepped it, lost my footing, and up-ended the tray onto the fake Persian carpet, missing the Princess's foot by a whisker!

Theodora reared up from the chair. "You clumsy woman!" she screamed. "You have no finesse! Look what you've done. My Persian rug – it's ruined!"

"It's alright … it's …"

"No, it's beyond repair. And look what you've done to poor Alastair!" She grabbed the unfortunate cat and clutched him to her as she began to wail. "My poor baby! She might have killed you!"

"Oh that's not true …"

"How would you know what's true?" She swung around to face me, the cat writhing in her arms. She put her face up close to mine. "You people without a life," she hissed, "You're so – so colourless!" She turned away, set the cat down and began to pace around the room. "Oh dear god in heaven, I can't stand it! It's all too much - too much!"

I stepped around her in shock, stooping to mop up the mess, hopping back and forth between the lounge and the kitchen, attempting to restore order.

An order of sorts was established before I left that day. But I wondered, as I let myself out of the flat, whether I would ever return. As I reached for the door handle, I could hear her muttering. "Oh, I'm so tired. And my head aches …" I felt a pang then. But I went ahead and closed the door behind me anyway.

It was coming on for summer when I heard the news. I was grocery shopping for my mother, when I ran into Sue, who was a mutual friend of mine and Theodora's.

The Princess had been very ill, Sue said. She'd finally gone to see a doctor who'd sent her for scans and, after much investigation, they'd found a tumour in her brain. It was the size of a pea. But her prospects of recovery were good, the doctors had said.

Joining the long self-checkout queue, I remembered all those mattresses. Recalled my last meeting with the Princess. How strange it was to think, that at the base of all that mayhem, lay something the size of a pea ...

I felt for the Princess and I did wish her a speedy recovery. She was such a survivor, I didn't doubt she'd emerge from this. And, maybe by now, the tale of the Princess and the Pea had found its way into her repertoire – perhaps, even with her great gift for embellishment, the pea had transformed into a small pumpkin!

But would I be there to hear about it? By the time I'd checked Mum's items through – the low-fat milk, the incontinence pads, the New Idea – I'd decided 'no'. Someone like the Princess would always find an audience. I had to find a life.

Another Siege

Judy de la Mare

A quiet spring Monday in leafy Karalee – a semi-rural suburb just fifteen minutes' drive to Ipswich city. All was calm except for the occasional noisy bird. Judy was reading an absorbing novel before starting some weeding in the garden which was always a job to be put off. She could hear the drone of a chopper above and at first thought nothing of it. Some thirty minutes later and it was still there. Looking outside she could see that it was circling over her house.

"How odd," she thought, "Maybe it was doing a survey or checking for fire-ants."

Standing on the side verandah which overlooked the house next door she saw a man lying in the grass – he was a policeman in body armour and was holding a gun. Her neighbour's dogs were jumping all over him thinking, no doubt, that he was playing a game with them. Judy ran to the fence and called to the dogs while the policeman ignored her. Suddenly the seriousness of the situation hit her and she ran inside.

"What was happening?" she thought as she opened the front door. Looking over her front fence were four more police officers. One called to her to get back inside and close the door, which she did. Still none the wiser as to what was going on, she decided to ring the police but they couldn't or wouldn't tell her anything.

An hour passed and peeking out a window she saw more armed police now on her neighbour's deck. Another

hour and an armoured vehicle arrived with camouflaged SWAT

officers. Her front gate opened and in they ran, pausing only to ask if her dog was inside. They had obviously noted the Beware of the Dog sign. After being assured, they continued on into her backyard and disappeared from view.

Judy has pet goats and was now concerned as the SWAT men had run in their direction, and also it was past their dinnertime. She loves her goats and spoils them with fruit and vegies. A policewoman had now approached and warned her that there was an armed man in the house next door to her neighbours and to stay inside.

By then the siege was well into its fourth hour and Judy decided to sneak down to the goat pen with their food. Staying low to the fence she crept down and opened the gate to their enclosure as quietly as she could. She had just entered when shouts erupted.

"Get down on the ground!" yelled a loud voice. That she did, looking up to see two puzzled goats looking at her. She then realised that the police were confronting the armed man and not shouting at her. She shakily got to her feet, fed the goats and walked back to the house in time to see the man in handcuffs being bundled into a police car.

All over thank goodness. It was her third siege in 35 years, all in different places. Hopefully it was her last!

Instructions III

Judy de la Mare

Firstly there can be several interpretations of this phrase. If one is angered and the nearest item at hand happens to be a pot it can be picked up and hurled. This commonly results in the pot being smashed and the anger of the person responsible can sometimes be lessened by doing this. Taking our frustrations out on inanimate objects can help to release tension. However this is not the technique that I will be describing today. In fact it is rather the complete opposite. I will tell you about a wonderful creative procedure of creating a pot of potential beauty from a lump of unattractive clay.

This term of "throwing a pot" comes from an old English word thrawan which means to twist or turn. To throw a pot you need to turn it on a wheel, which can be driven by your foot, called a kick wheel, or by electricity, which is an electric wheel. I have used both and though the kick wheel can give better speed control it also requires a lot of strength. I wonder if the medieval potter would have stood out in a crowd by being the man with huge muscles only in his right leg. I did not persevere long enough with a kick wheel to test this theory.

Today we will work with an electric wheel and begin by first preparing our clay. This is kneaded, very much like kneading bread dough, and the object is to remove all air bubbles. A good workout can be achieved by this, in fact the whole procedure is good for your body.

Next the clay is rolled into a ball shape and placed on the centre of the wheel. It is best to throw it there with some force while having the wheel turning fast. This is done with a foot pedal. Wet your hands and the clay and then squeeze it into a tower shape. You may remember the scene from Ghost when Demi Moore was distracted by Patrick Swayze whilst working at the wheel. It is best not to have such distractions when creating a pot! – although when the pot is finished you may invite an admirer in. After achieving a conical shape it is then pushed down using both hands firmly. This is repeated 3 or 4 times to help centre the clay.

Centreing means that the outer edges are perfectly smooth. Your mind as well as your body must be centred over the wheel to attain this. Cup the clay in both hands, making sure that they are still wet and start smoothing the clay with your palms. Some peaceful music played during this can enhance the ability to stay attuned to the magic of wheel throwing.

Once the clay is centred and not wobbling about, it is time to open it. Push down in the middle with your forefinger straight into the spinning clay, stopping about 2cm from the bottom. While doing this your other hand acts as a stabilizer. Then slowly remove your finger. Speaking of fingers – nails must be very short and it is best not to wear rings.

To enlarge the hole, reinsert your finger and brace the outer wall with your other hand. Add other fingers as the hole widens. Now compress the bottom with your fingers or use a wooden thumb, which is a useful potter's tool.

If all this has gone to plan we are getting close to the end. We must now raise the walls of the pot, unless we are making an ashtray or a dog bowl. The pot will be very wet so we use a sponge here, pressing it with your index finger and, lifting them up to thin the walls, and make them higher. Not too thin or it will collapse. Not too thick or it will be too heavy. Wheel throwing is a bit like walking a tightrope – too fast and you will fall, too slow and you will also fall. Or in the case of the pot it will fall apart.

Now even out the top as it is probably a bit rough. Use a pin projecting from a wooden cylinder and while the wheel is slowly turning, press it into the clay at the top and when it is completely cut all the way round it can be removed. You have just made a basic cylinder which can be further enhanced with handles, a spout or a lid. Then it can be painted with underglazes - there are hundreds of different ways to decorate a pot. It is all up to your imagination, before it finally goes into the kiln for firing and comes out as work of art!

Answer: See Appendix on page 132

Chicken Kiev

Joan Alexander

Chicken Kiev was the meal that a boyfriend and I shared on our first date together. I was an unsophisticated 18 year old and was thrilled with the invitation to an upmarket Sydney city restaurant. My previous outings with friends had been to pubs featuring jazz bands, or to the local restaurant and coffee shop in Newtown. So this was a red letter evening. I chose the 'Chicken Kiev' on his advice. As this was the first time I had heard of this dish, I was interested enough to ask whether it was a recent addition to the restaurant's menu. Well, it was as if the flood gates opened, and that night I learned more than enough about this dish!

Chicken Kiev is a chicken fillet pounded and rolled around butter, garlic and herbs then coated with egg and breadcrumbs and fried or baked. My friend said it would be a taste sensation, but to be very careful when first piercing the fillet with your fork. On no account aim for the centre because you may well be sprayed with hot garlic and herb butter. Always commence at the smaller end, thus gently releasing some of the hot contents. Very good advice!

Its origin was in the 18th century, part of the repertoire of a French chef. As French chefs were hired by Russian gentry, Russian chefs adopted many French haute cuisine traditions. In 1818 the famous chef, Careme, spent several months in St Petersburg at the Court of Alexander. His short time there had a profound impact on Russian cuisine in general.

In 1897 a luxury hotel was built in the centre of Kiev. This was the Continental Hotel. It was a beautiful building, and became very popular, and when its signature dish Chicken Kiev was introduced, it became an immediate success, and ensured that its popularity would continue into the 20th century. In 1941 the Wehrmacht, the Nazi army invaded the Soviet Union and occupied Kiev. The Continental hotel was mined and blown up, killing many of the invaders who had taken over the hotel. Finally, post-war, the luxury hotel was rebuilt in 1955. Hopefully Chicken Kiev remains on its menu.

Ever since that evening I have enjoyed Chicken Kiev on many occasions, but seldom with a companion with such a flow of eloquence.

Softly Spoken Words

Philip J Bradbury

Simon would later declare "I was not the speaker but the words were given me,".

It happened at a time when he felt his least courageous, his least capable. His most vulnerable. All was not well in the home; the ex-husband was abusive, the step son was taking drugs and other people's things – cars, mainly – and Simon was being forced back to the occupation he hated with a passion because his book sales weren't enough to satisfy a wife who wanted more. Actually, his book sales weren't enough to feed his pet snail! So, what with having to bail out someone else's son, bail up someone else's husband, live in fear of the bailiff bailing him up and to bail out of his dream of making a difference with words to live someone else's dream, he wondered where the word success applied to his life. Besides, the prospect of another failed marriage set him thinking he was genetically incapable of loving and being loved.

A tougher man would have sorted it. A real bloke would have stood up to the mark (or whatever real blokes do) and just dealt with it. Unflinching. Without emotion. He would have punched his way through and proudly told his mates about it over another round of beers.

Not so our soft man who won all his fights by a hundred yards. Having been brought up amid abuse and weekly beatings, his distaste for conflict equalled his distaste for accounting, the drudgery he was being forced back into while his dreams fluttered as burnt ash in the winter storm.

He took it all to heart, kept it to himself, pretended he was coping and quietly shrank inside.

It was only a small incident – one he can never recall – but it was the last of a thousand shards to pierce his tyres and flatten his soul. The looks of derision from his wife and step daughter are still etched in his peripheral mind. Maybe he'd bought a candy bar for himself and not them or something ... something small it was and their looks of disgust that tipped the balance.

There seemed no way out and it overwhelmed him. His feet took him from the house, along the estuary boardwalk and to the sea ... and into the sea, into which he would have kept walking had the voice not called to him. The chilly winter water shocked his flat mind awake and something inside beseeched him stop. It was as if the massive Hand of God was at his back, turning him. He obeyed and sat on a washed-up log, contemplating the expansive sea, forever moving and getting nowhere.

Just like him.

But the voice arose and he couldn't explain its source or its nature. It was, perhaps, a knowing, intangible and undeniable. Not an excitement but a contentment. A quietly persistent surge of something he knew but couldn't explain. The brush with death had awaken life and it stirred quietly in his bowels, his stomach and rose as tears to his eyes. He sat and cried tears of release for what he knew not, for the longest time, and finally smiled.

Rising from the log, he patted it with a gratitude he hadn't felt for years. Forever perhaps. He walked back to the house and nothing touched him. No fear. No joy. No excitement. No judgement. Feeling inert and strangely powerful he ignored his wife's demands to know his whereabouts and closed the door to his office. Something other than his tiny self took his hand, took up his pen and he wrote ... and wrote and wrote.

He would normally have read it back and edited it but he knew it was fine as it was. And, if it wasn't fine, if it was a little cracked, then that's where the light could shine through.

The first of these stories he posted on his blog. He sat back and smiled. Nothing happened.

He clicked into his email and there was an invitation from a Dianne Lang, asking him to speak at an international AIDS conference in Port

Elizabeth, South Africa. He immediately replied Yes, never having heard of Dianne Lang or Port Elizabeth before. He realised he knew nothing about AIDS but he had eight months to research it.

He got out his old guitar and raised money for the trip by busking each week, while accounting paid the daily bills till the divorce came through.

His three months in South Africa were transformative; speaking at the conference, co-facilitating AIDS workshops with Dianne in the townships in the Big Karoo and meeting people whose inspiration was as high as the depths of the squalour from which they came. He was never the same again.

And the stories he put up on his blog? Two women – one from Canada and one from England – eventually emailed him to say that one of his stories inspired them to think again and not to end their lives. Many other emails thanked him, telling him his words touched people in many different ways.

It served to remind him that our dreams do, indeed, come true but seldom in the way we imagine. They were simple words but no less effective for gentleness.

A Walk in the Woods

Paul Howlett

The hard snow crunched under my feet as I walked from the little sleepy village and cautiously entered the wooded area at the end of the street.

These woods looked beautiful in the cold night air. There was no wind and the night seemed quiet and serene.

I was on my way to visit an old lady who lived in the woods. She was a relative of mine that I had not seen for several weeks and I was concerned that she may be ill. I came prepared to give her some of my nice cookies, which I had baked that morning. I know she always loves my cookies.

My solar powered torch was powerful and showed up the winding track between the old oak trees. The trees looked very old and a little sinister in the beam of light, but my footsteps were firm on the frosty snow, as I had on my favourite snow boots.

The time it took to walk the distance to my relative's humble house was about half an hour during the daytime, but at night it took much longer. The snow seemed to get deeper with each step that I took and I wondered if I should wait for tomorrow to make the journey.

Then I heard the cry of some animals in the woods. The sound sent a shiver down my spine and I hastened my steps. This whole journey seemed now to be a bad idea. I was not afraid, just concerned that I would have to confront something that I had prepared for, but did not want to experience.

I walked on deeper into the forest.

My skirt snagged on a protruding branch and left a sliver of material draped in its leaves. I zipped up my coat to make sure that I did not get hung up on any more trees. The moon was due to appear in a short time and I wanted to be safe in the cabin before the woods were lit up by the bright cold magical moonlight.

In the distance I could hear the sounds of the wild wolves that lived in the forest. I was not afraid of these animals. I did not want to meet them tonight, but I was prepared to face them if they found me.

Ten minutes later I heard the sound of animals behind me, the howls of the wild wolves was very low, loud and getting stronger. I was not happy!

The wolf pack was in full cry coming down the track and following close behind me. I knew I had to confront the wolves. I turned and looked back to find that … the alpha male wolf was only a few metres behind me.

I was angry. I was furious. I need to be inside my grandmother's house and not out with the moon due to rise overhead in the near future.

The alpha male wolf sat up and looked at me with hungry eyes. I stared right back.

"How dare you interrupt my visit to my grandmother?" I said to him.

The wolf replied with a telepathic message, that we want you - now.

I responded with a thought that made the leader of the pack cringe. I mentally shouted to him the full fury of my mind. The wolf pack did not move, and they were blocking the path to the cabin, that was now just out of reach. I was running out of time.

The moon started to rise about the tree line and I could feel the cold dark influence seep throughout my body. I tried to walk past the pack and make it to the safety of my grandmother's cabin, but all in vain.

I had three large wolves hanging on to the end of my red coat and I knew that they would not let go. I was now more than angry as the wolves were ruining my good red cloak! I would need to repair it in the morning.

The moon rose higher in the sky and the wolf pack had won the fight. I was doomed to run with the pack tonight. Something I did not want to do this month.

I could feel my body changing as the moonlight strengthened. Hair started to grow all over my body and my basket of cookies fell to the ground as I lost the ability to grip the handle. My hands turned into paws and my body changed to a large female werewolf. I was not happy because I would not have morphed into a wolf this month, if I had made it to grandma's cabin.

Now I had to run with the pack for the whole night!!

I just hope that I do not get pregnant!!

The Yellow Satin Boxers

Janet Findlay

I could tell you about an incident that was embarrassing beyond belief. Actually, it wasn't the time I was charging through LAX to catch a connecting flight with a pair of my old knickers dangling from my suitcase. No, it was more embarrassing than that – though it did involve pants. This toe-curling mishap occurred later in my life – in the course of my career as a clown.

Aha, I can almost hear someone saying, "A career as a clown? Well, what do you expect then? Don't you generate embarrassing incidents if you're a clown? Isn't that part of your stock in trade? Aren't you either trained or predisposed to make a fool of yourself? And perhaps you even become immune to embarrassment?"

Yes, yes - that's all that's true to a point. But as we know, in life, a random factor can often come into play. A wild card, a cat among the pigeons that can blow our expectations and best preparations to smithereens. And this embarrassing incident was SO out of the box, they didn't even imagine it happening when I studied Clowning 101.

In fact, this occurrence was so bad that it put paid to my clowning career for once and for all and I have only ever shared this incident – apart from the 30 people who had the bad fortune to witness it –with one other human being on the planet; my partner, Rick.

Whenever I want to shake him out of his easy-going complacency, I refer to the incident known between us as The Yellow Satin Boxers, and delight in watching him put his head in his hands and begin to squirm. If I begin to recount it in detail, he'll look up and beg me to stop. He's practically pleaded with me not to share this with anyone else. Hmmmn. We'll see.

But before, or indeed, if I do share this story, I really want to look at what has predisposed me to a lifetime of embarrassing incidents. For the episode of The Yellow Satin Boxers merely sits at the top of a mountain of such events.

I've asked myself many questions over the years. Could it be that I'm hard-wired to embarrassment? That somewhere in my DNA lurks the gene for public shame? Is it possible that an Irish ancestor on my mother's side – a certain Tom Scanlon who left his wife and eleven kids in County Clare to pursue a carefree life as a vaudeville artist in the colonies, may have passed down this gene down to me … when he married a publican's widow in Sydney and had to endure a humiliating public trial for bigamy?

I guess I'll never know. So since I can't prove the DNA theory, I'm more inclined to trace the source of my Greatest Embarrassments, to an incident that occurred early in my own life.

My mother Cushla Veronica, was a strong, proud woman who wanted fame, fortune and a large family. She was ahead of her time in that she wanted it all. But things being what they were after World War 11, she had to settle for the large family.

She and my father, Leonard Stanley, didn't have good communication it seemed. Perhaps just as much as was necessary to generate that large family, and from then on, to support it. There never seemed to be much money, but as Rick likes to point out, we did own a beach house (as well as my mother's family home) and we used to holiday there at every opportunity.

In January 1953, Cushla Veronica must really have needed that holiday. Six months earlier she'd given birth to a stillborn child she'd named Margaret Mary, and my father had apparently gone into a cone of silence. Unwilling or incapable of even talking to her about it, let alone offering comfort.

So there we were one day in that tepid New Zealand summer, swimming at Tangimoana Beach – where even the name means the Crying of the Sea - and my poor mother was sitting on the grey, gritty shore reading a book, trying to drown her sorrows in the story of some famous person's life. Regularly she would look up from the page, and account for her five living children, frolicking in the shallow waves. I was the youngest.

From my point of view, the beach was sheer enjoyment, the play of waves and sea spray sent me into giggles of delight. I loved it. And I wanted more. I wanted the beach ball that I knew was in the boot of Mum's old black Austin which was parked behind a sand hill. I knew that if I had that red and yellow ball to throw into the waves, my enjoyment would be complete.

I can remember getting the ball out of the car boot – quite an achievement for a three-year-old I see now! But I can't remember what took me to the top of the sand dune overlooking the beach. Was it the single haunting cry that suddenly rang out – or was it the rising sound of a general commotion? I do remember standing wide-eyed next to Nellie Watson, our neighbour, as we witnessed my mother threshing around in the waves, fully-dressed, screaming out "My baby, my baby – I've lost you!" and then watching her wade deeper and deeper into the ocean. I stood as still as a fat little cherub statue, the beach ball clasped to my tummy, and looked on uncomprehending as people ran in to the water and dragged out my mother – soaking wet and wailing.

Then out of the blue, someone looked up and noticed me. My mother swung around and stretched her arms out from the shore, mouthing something I couldn't hear. Then it seemed all eyes were upon me.

At my side, I heard a low angry voice. "Look what you've made your mother go through! Making such a spectacle of herself!" I heard and understood what Nellie Watson was saying. At three and a half though, I wasn't sure that I wanted to buy into it. Why was I to blame for this sudden explosion of drama and public shame? All I'd wanted was a beach ball to play with in the waves … and girls just want to have fun after all!

But Nellie was a grown up. And grown-ups knew everything. They knew what was right, and what was wrong and who was to blame for things. I looked up at Nellie with her harsh glare and crimson slash of lipstick, and I took it on. Then and there, I accepted that I had been the sole cause of my mother's pain and subsequent embarrassment. But I knew I didn't like Nellie Watson … and I never looked her in the eye again.

Cushla Veronica was so relieved and overwhelmed to be united with her youngest living child that she never accused me of behaving badly. But I had made my decision to take the blame and from then on things changed.

Because all our decisions have consequences. One consequence of this was, I never learned to swim. And I became famous in our family for my lack of initiative. But the main consequence and the one that is relevant here, was that, as the years went by, I would find myself being the public face of humiliation and embarrassment. For example, I was the child who stood up in class and confessed to a plot against the teacher, a plot that all the kids had been party to. Unnecessary confessions became my thing.

I was also attracted to situations that held a high risk factor for embarrassment. I was the student who 'dried' during the Senior speech contest, and ran panicking from the stage only to return and do it again!

So you can see that such acts of masochism led inevitably and seamlessly to my career as a clown, a career where embarrassing incidents become your currency. A career where, behind a white face and a painted crimson slash of a smile, you put yourself forward as a scapegoat for all the foibles and follies of our kind. (Or so you may think at grandiose moments.)

You may even fool yourself that you are controlling the situation, that you're holding the power, because, after all, it's you who throws down the banana skin for yourself to skid on. It's you who allows the kids to pull on your red nose.

But was I really exercising a choice every time? Or was I still caught up in the echoing reverberation of that first choice – that of accepting to be the Public Cause of my mother's pain and shame.

In hindsight, I see it's a good thing that the incident of the Yellow Satin Boxers came along to mortify me. For it halted the escalating momentum of my public foolery, and allowed me to choose a rather more edifying and private life path.

And will I now disclose the details of that Most Embarrassing Incident of my adult existence? No way! Apart from airing it occasionally, to discomfort my more conservative partner, I keep the Terrible Tale of the Yellow Satin Boxer Shorts close to my chest. And I'm pleased to say that, finally, that's okay with me.

Westwood Towers

Paul Howlett.

The people who had to work in Westwood towers hated the building. It had been quickly constructed by a firm that was on the verge of bankruptcy. The builders cut costs wherever they could, as later reports were to confirm that this building was in a very sorry state.

When the wind blew and the rain battered the windows of Westwood Towers some of the windows leaked. The water would seep in and drip from the light fittings, making them dangerous and, most of the time, unworkable.

One report by a building inspector read as follows:

1. The windows of the Westwood Tower are not up to Australian Standard No 5967 as they are ill fitting and internally weak.
2. The air conditioning is faulty as it ceases to work for ten hours per week in many levels of the building.
3. The elevators are in need of repair and a major overhaul.

The newspapers reported a terrifying ordeal for some of the office workers in Westwood Towers. The elevator number five gave a lunch time crowd of people a ride from hell. Our source confirmed that he had used lift number 5 to exit the building at noon for lunch. The lift doors had failed to open and the lift made several journeys up and down the whole twenty five floors of the building. On exiting the lift our informant had warned the people entering the lift to not use it as it is not working correctly.

Screams were heard from Lift No 5 as the elevator rapidly ascended and descended without stopping for the next half hour. Some of the occupants of the lift fainted, and some vomited as the lift yo-yoed till the emergency workers stopped the faulty elevator.

Parliamentary sources confirmed that the local government was very concerned about the safety of office workers who have to use this building on a daily basis. A special investigation was setup to look into every aspect of the safety issues.

Workers in the building still had to go to work and the investigation turned out to be another local government cover up.

Westwood Towers still exists today under a new name and a new owner. The Public Service office workers were relocated to a new building several blocks away and Westwood Towers had a total refit for the new owners.

There have been no bad reports in the press with the new owners.

The Sacrifice Is Accepted

Mark Grieveson

"Chickens, we need more white chickens to avert further catastrophes". The speaker of these ominous words was Marie, a wizened voodoo mambo of indeterminate years. Three weeks earlier, Port-au-Prince had been ravaged by a 7.2 earthquake that collapsed most of its buildings, destroyed the water supply and killed thousands of people.

Aftershocks still racked the city but cholera was now the main concern. The limited medical services were overwhelmed by the scale of the disaster and more people were dying every day.

Marie's clan was reduced to hoping their well-practiced age old voodoo rituals would avert further deaths in her clan. Already nineteen of her vodooists had perished.

Traditionally the sacrifice of chickens had been sufficient propitiation to the invisibles, the intermediaries between Bondye, the supreme unknowable creator and humans. Despite several recent ceremonies, the tutelary spirits had rejected their entreaties and failed to avert the spread of the dreaded disease.

Marie was in a privileged position as mambo as she was supported by her clan. But she sensed their allegiance was waning as more and more fell ill. Thus she decided on one supreme ceremony, never before seen in the lifetime of any of those present.

She had her acolyte Celine prepare the secret mixture which diminished the will of the participants and enabled them to gyrate for many hours without tiring. Its active ingredients were an extract of puffer fish toxin and crushed datura seeds, the plant known as witches weed in the middle-ages. The effects of ingesting this potion was the source of zombie folklore. Celine was a mulatto girl in her mid-twenties, tall with a flawless complexion - indeed more than once she had been called a dusky beauty.

Now, she secretly harboured the opinion that she would make a better mambo than Marie and that the invisibles would (like the men in her village) respect her obvious qualities. As she sharpened the sacrificial machete, she imagined it cutting Marie's throat rather than that of an underfed chicken. She obsessed over how she might be able to do it and, more importantly, get away with it. She viewed it as an entree to a life of relative ease, far better than toiling in her father's hot laundry every day.

The time of the big ceremony arrived. The company removed themselves to the sacred waterfall under which they symbolically washed away their sins. Their present practice had wisely incorporated much of what the Catholic priests had taught them over the centuries.

Thusly shriven, they repaired to the adjacent ceremonial ground where persistent scrubbings had failed to entirely obliterate the traces of blood from previous sacrifices. They each imbibed of the sacred mixture and commenced dancing to the steady beat of African rhythms brought over in the slave ships.

The slow ritual dance and the drink combined weaved its spell and person after person entered the liminal state of consciousness that signified access to the invisibles. Celine led the dance and was handed chicken after chicken. She deftly cut the throat of each and whirled around faster and faster holding the sacrifices one by one by the legs and spraying blood over the white clothing of the gathering.

The frenzy had begun and Celine as the main participant started to vocalize messages from the other world. By intent, she had drunk very little of the mixture. Her glossolalia became more insistent that she, Celine, should be made Mambo if the contagion was to stop.

Upon hearing this from the sidelines, Marie grew strangely calm and entered a deeper state than ever before. It was as if she became one of the invisibles herself and that the gathering was under her control.

Faster and faster Celine whirled in an unearthly frenzy spewing a mixture of blood and sweat on the others who despite the drug started to pause and view the unnatural display.

Suddenly she dropped to the ground dead.

Marie voicing the will of the invisibles intoned, "The sacrifice is accepted," in a model of laconic eloquence.

The Dirt Bike

NK

In 1968, when I was 20, I bought a Honda 50cc step-through motorbike.

I thought I was the ants pants.

I rode to the police station in Liverpool to go for my licence.

The police station was in the backblocks of Liverpool, on a dirt road.

As I did a u-turn to pull up in front of the station my bike skidded and I fell off.

Right in front of six policemen who were lined up on the verandah, having their afternoon smok-o.

Blush.

Bella's Gift

NK

Bella was one of those people who was sure that nothing bad would ever happen to her. She knew she would never have a car accident, never have a major illness, not die of cancer and certainly not have a flooded house – even though it had been flooded once before; but she didn't live in it then. So imagine her shock when her house was flooded in 2011. She first heard about her house being flooded from a friend a 100 miles away!

Said friend rang her and in sympathetic voice crooned, "I hear your house is flooded."

"No," replied Bella, "the rain stopped last night and it would have all flowed away. I don't think so."

So, after a leisurely breakfast at the house of the friend who had given her shelter from a possible flood (not that it was going to happen, but best to be sure) she drove jauntily round to her house to see that all was well.

As she turned into her street she saw her house roof sitting just above the water. At first she couldn't take it in. She just looked at it, stunned. Her brain pushed it away as an illusion. Then she began to sob. She stood in the street, sobbing, hiccuping. Looking and not looking. Expecting that the picture would change if she stood very still, that she wasn't really seeing what she was seeing.

In a very few minutes the sticky summer heat and the shock became too much. She needed to sit and it was too hot to sit on the road, so she went into a neighbour's front yard and sat on his front steps, looking at her house, still not believing her eyes, still sobbing. There was no way of taking it in. Then other possibilities presented themselves. What if she'd stayed in the house? What if the flood had come up during the night and she was trapped in her bedroom? There would have been no way out then. She would have jumped out of the window into a raging torrent. No chance to get on the roof from that room. She would have drowned. "Drama queen," she chided herself. But really she wasn't a drama queen, she really would have drowned.

The house was high set at the front, and low set at the back. Her bedroom was in the high set part and if she had gone to sleep convinced that all was well and the house had filled up from the back, by the time it got to her bedroom, egress would have been blocked off. Injury, if not drowning, would have been certain. Jumping out of the window – if indeed that had been possible – would have hurled her into a river a mile wide carrying all sorts of debris – doors and pallets, trees and rubbish bins, possibly animals, possibly snakes – all the strange debris she found later on, hanging in trees and perched on bushes (including an aviary which came to rest on her nature strip), after the waters subsided.

So there she is, sitting on a neighbour's step, sobbing, looking at her lovely house submerged in brown water; only the roof showing.

The day was hot and very humid. The sun stung and there was a peculiar stillness. Still because the roads were cut and no traffic hummed on the nearby highway. No lawn mowers, no motor bikes, no people talking or shouting or laughing, no blaring televisions or music. The suburb was hushed. There was no electricity. It felt a little like the end of the world. Indeed it was for the moment - the end of Bella's world as she realised she was now officially homeless.

She loved that house, she loved this suburb and although she had a little money, it wasn't enough to start again. Her thoughts churned.

Over the next 24 hours the water subsided, leaving three inches of mud on the driveway – thick and sticky and slippery. It was impossible to walk to the back door without slipping and sliding.

Bella's neighbour across the road managed to wade up the drive and push open the back door – a chip board cupboard had fallen against it, making it difficult to open - but Ross was young and strong and persuaded the door to let him in.

There was more mud covering the polished wooden floor. The large bookshelves had buckled and spilled their contents onto the floor. A glass fronted cupboard had toppled over and china (unbroken!) lay scattered in the mud. A shelf with precious pottery had fallen forwards and spilled its contents onto the floor – again, unbroken but occasionally chipped.

The white lounge was saturated with muddy water and smaller pieces of furniture lay at crazy angles.

A friend's son arrived with a Gerni and started to hose off the driveway and the side of the house. Pretty quickly local, unaffected residents of the suburb arrived to begin the clean up.

The next morning it began in earnest. People arrived from Boonah. Locals came. People from Beaudesert came. People came with Gernis, and trucks, and buckets and mops and rags. People came with cleaning products and leather gloves. It was the most amazing thing.

Later Bella found out that a friend had sent round an email to all their mutual friends, telling them of the disaster and asking for help. They came in droves.

First to be cleaned was the toilet – the walls covered in mud, the toilet itself unusable.

Simultaneously, Bella begged the volunteers, "Save my kitchen," so they set about emptying cupboards and drying the shelves, washing the contents, wiping mud out of joins and handles.

Other volunteers took out the furniture. Some of it had to go straight to the tip, some of it was rescuable. The wooden furniture was hosed off. The large mat was hung over the fence and hosed and hosed and hosed. (Although there was no electricity, thank heavens they hadn't turned off the water.)

There were funny things too. The wooden kitchen table had floated and the all the papers left on top were exactly as Bella had left them! The wooden bed also floated although the mattress absorbed water.

Over the next week new people came every day. At one point Bella had to turn them away – the house was too small to accommodate any more volunteers!

And why did they come? Why did they keep coming? Bella asked one family why and they said they felt bad for the victims, they felt glad it hadn't happened to them, they wanted to help so they just got in the car and drove to a suburb they knew was flooded – and they ended up at Bella's house. No one sent them, no one coordinated them. They just came.

Another local resident took video footage and gave Bella a copy.

Bella's brother came and worked on her electricity, her sister-in-law took home armfuls of clothes and linen to wash. They washed windows and bookshelves and little bits of jewellery.

Bella's friend Alice (who gave her shelter from the flood) washed and washed and washed. She even cleaned Bella's collection of soft toys. And every night she cooked Bella a two course nourishing meal and gave her a clean place to live – for three weeks. That's friendship.

Others offered to wash blankets and sheets and jumpers and for a while Bella's household goods were spread over Ipswich.

For weeks afterward people came to the door asking if Bella needed help or offering clothes, linen and toiletries.

And many weeks later a friend came and washed all of Bella's DVDs and CDs (and most them played fine).

The mud was amazing. For weeks you could see the floodline in the trees and bushes. Strange 'sculptures' revealed themselves – a part of a fence hung with rags, some pallets adorned with pieces of decking and toilet paper (don't think about it); some orange plastic safety fencing hung metres up from a gum tree and paper was flung everywhere.

Six years later Bella still finds flood mud – in the wheels of her tea trolley, at the back of a chest of drawers.

She welcomes those little reminders because this wasn't a disaster. This was an enormous, enormous affirmation of the kindness of strangers, the staunchness of friendships and even the willingness of bureaucrats to ease the way of the 'victims'.

Bella doesn't feel like a victim, she feels like she received a gift.

H and G Pharmaceuticals

Mark Grieveson

Most of us know the story of Hansel and Gretel from the 1812 fairy tale version by the Grimm brothers. Some may even be familiar with the wonderful 1893 opera by Engelbert Humperdinck. Yes he's the composer whose name was misappropriated by one Arnold Dorsey in the 1960s, thereby reversing his lack of hit records. What a difference a name makes!

In the original highly moralistic tale, Hansel and Gretel are a young brother and sister kidnapped by a cannibalistic witch living deep in the forest in a house constructed of cake and confectionery – I kid you not. The two children save their lives by outwitting her and, I might add, burning her to death. They stole her cache of gold coins and save their father from a life of poverty. Such stories were the early 19th century equivalent of today's aspirational Gold Lotto draws. The evil stepmother who was the cause of their expulsion from the bosom of the family had conveniently died while they were on their adventures. It's little wonder children of the past were especially prone to nightmares.

So let's see … there is the obligatory wicked stepmother, the ineffectual father and children wiser than their elders – three mischievous archetypes that persist into our own allegedly more enlightened century.

But it's high time that the real tale was told.

Firstly Hansel and Gretel were first class brats, juvenile delinquents in the making. Their birth mother having died, their father married again in an attempt to provide a supportive home life for his children.

There was no school or other children to interact with in such an isolated position in the woods.

His new wife tried to instil some discipline, culture and manners into the home. She was resisted, resented and sabotaged at every turn. The father usually took the children's side and the wife gradually stopped eating and fell into a deep depression. So now the children found her boring as well as tyrannical. They were in those dangerous middle teenage years, that age when present teenagers want tattoos and high tech entertainment to stem their existential angst. With their father away most of the day cutting wood, they decided they were old enough to set out on their own to find a more stimulating life.

They left a barely legible note for their father, packed some food and a few belongings and confidently strode off into the unknown. After two days of wandering, and with their bread gone, they espied a cottage with smoke rising from the chimney. It was backed by a large well-tended garden with tall green aromatic plants.

Their knock was answered by an ancient crone (a word unfortunately derived from the old French word Carogne, meaning carrion). It has two distinct connotations viz:

1) a hag, and

2) a woman who is venerated for her experience, judgment, and wisdom. The latter meaning applies in this instance.

She was of indeterminate age though obviously advanced in years and, noticing their depleted condition, invited them in. Once they were seated, she produced a plate of brownies and a jug of milk. The children gorged themselves on the food, too hungry to notice a curious backtaste. After twenty minutes or so, they felt calmer than they ever had before and the old lady suggested she show them around. Once outside they were overwhelmed by the light. Indeed everything seemed to have an innate mellow glow and the cottage looked candy coloured.

It transpired that, in certain quarters, the old lady was considered a witch. Whenever I hear that word, I am immediately reminded of the immortal dialogue from the 1954 movie Brigadoon:

Mr Lundie: Two hundred years ago, the highlands of Scotland were plagued with witches, wicked sorcerers that were taking the Scottish people away from the teachings of God and putting the Devil into their souls. They were indeed horrible destructive women. I dinna suppose you have such women in your country?

Tommy Albright: Witches?

Jeff Douglas: Oh we have 'em. We just pronounce it differently.

But I digress. She really was what we might today call a herbalist. An only child, she inherited the cottage and her mother's handwritten books containing wide knowledge of the healing properties of plants, the Tarot and other forms of divination. People consulted her for advice on their aches and pains, their fortune and their love lives. They paid only what they could afford. Never marrying, she devoted herself to furthering her mother's investigation into the arcana.

From her wide experience, she recognized Hansel and Gretel as suffering from the 19th century equivalent of ADHD and knew that the special ingredient of the brownies would calm them down. Indeed, after their exploration of the premises, they felt hungrier than ever.

Over some fruit, she elicited their story and knew she would have to contact their father. By dint of questioning those who sought her counsel, she found out where he resided and sent a message to let him know his children were safe and well. It transpired that his new wife had died by her own hand, misunderstood by both husband and stepchildren.

She was getting on in age and invited the children to live with her. After the stepmother's funeral, their father joined them and tended the gardens which was much easier on his aging bones than woodcutting.

Over time the children, especially Hansel, became interested in her ideas, thereby discovering that the secret of life is to be really passionate about something.

Gretel eventually married and lived in a newly built adjacent cottage. She had three children whose antics blessed the declining years of both their grandfather and of the crone.

Hansel meanwhile discovered he possessed an innate business sense and started a family company which has since extended worldwide.

H and G Pharmaceuticals today has branches everywhere and is actively lobbying Western governments to decriminalize marijuana so they can take full advantage of their two hundred years expertise in its properties and use.

The Ant and the Grasshopper

NK

The days were getting shorter and the air a little chillier and the leaves had turned red and yellow; some had even fallen to the ground. But the days were still warm, the bees still buzzed and the little black ants worked busily, collecting food and taking it deep into the earth.

The grasshopper sat in the warm early autumn sun and played his merry fiddle. His fingers had been a little stiff with cold that morning, but that was easy to ignore as the sun rose in the sky and warmed the stones at his back. When he was hungry he nibbled a leaf and was a little surprised to find that it tasted stale, a little old and lifeless. "Oh well" he thought, "autumn is here, the leaves are drying up – I'll try a blade of grass instead".

As he sat chewing and enjoying the sunshine he noticed a little ant carefully carrying a piece of dead insect.

The ant was balancing a huge leg of cockroach in its front legs and every now and then the leg grew too heavy and the ant had to rest. Occasionally the ant overbalanced, dropping the leg and looking so comical that the grasshopper laughed and played a happy riff on his violin. "Why do you work so hard little ant, there is plenty of food," asked the grasshopper.

"Winter is coming and it is growing cold", said the Ant. "When the snow comes, food will be hard to find and my feet will freeze if I go out. I am laying by a store of food so that I will be snug and safe until next spring."

"Do you never dance or sing little ant?" asked the grasshopper. "Not I," said the ant "I am too busy for frivolity, life is hard and summer is short, I must work or how will I survive?"

"Life is hard and summer is short," repeated the grasshopper musingly. "That is why I sing and dance all summer long," he laughed, "because life is hard and summer is short and I will enjoy it whilst I can. I have never lacked for food."

"But what will you do when winter comes?" cried the little ant.

"I will sing and dance," replied the grasshopper carelessly, but it gave him pause nonetheless.

The little ant too had food for thought. "It's true," she thought, "I never sing and dance, and oh! How lovely his fiddle sounds and how my feet long to dance." So she trudged on, dragging and pulling and pushing, first a seed, then a crumb, then an insect, then an unnameable something that smelled good to eat. But every now and then she skipped a little, in something that looked a bit like a dance step. The grasshopper saw her and smiled. But he too had food for thought.

The days got shorter, the leaves grew more bitter, the grass turned yellow. And still the little ant worked, and the grasshopper fiddled his merry tunes. Each watched the other thinking, thinking. The grasshopper grew a little thinner each day as food became scarce. The ant grew a little more morose each day as the days got colder and darker. Finally, one day, she sighed sadly and her shoulders drooped as she realised that soon she would not hear the fiddle any more. The grasshopper sighed too, realising that soon it would grow too cold and he would have no food when the snow came. His fingers grew stiffer each day with the cold, and they rarely warmed up properly now to play his fastest tunes.

On the last and bitterest day of autumn the ant found the grasshopper near death from cold and starvation. His fiddle lay nearby, clouded with chilly dew, silent now, but still full of happy memories. The ant almost cried for lack of the merry tunes that had filled her working days with rhythm and the promise of dance. The grasshopper almost cried because he had come to admire this industrious little ant as she dragged her amazing burdens past him.

"C'est la vie," breathed the grasshopper who had learned a little French from a snail, and composed himself for the inevitable.

"C'est la NOT vie," cried the ant suddenly. "Come and live with me! You shall play your fiddle and I shall learn to dance the dark winter through. And you will share my food. So we will both be satisfied."

And so they did! And so they were!

The Emperor's New Clothes

Mark Grieveson

"Apparel oft proclaims the man" or so the bard has said
But in this benighted day, tattoos are more au fait;
For on some torsos volumes may be read.

Thoughts clothe the mind; sans them, one's considered dim
But that's no impediment to becoming US president.
The Emperor's New Clothes could have been written for him.

Freeflowing hair, sky deliriously blue
Yellow hippie skirt, faded cheesecloth shirt
Aquarian perfection - Nimbin 1972

When we view old movies circa 1976
Chuck Norris wears flares and everyone stares
In utter disbelief - how could we have been such hicks?

Old TV garb make us laugh
Widow's weeds, Miss Marple's tweeds
And Dr Who's coat and scarf

Hansel and Gretel - A Fairy Tale

Jenny Chriswick

Once upon a time there was a wood cutter and his wife who were very troubled. It had been a very bad year and there was a famine. They were down to their last loaf of bread. The man was not one to be defeated and at least they were warm tonight and had a roof over their heads.

"Children," he said, "tomorrow morning we will rise early and go into the woods and chop more firewood and find mushrooms to eat." Hansel and Gretel had never been to the woods with their parents before and it would be fun so they were very happy.

So the woodcutter, his wife and the two children set off early next morning and marched into the dense forest. It was several hours before they found a suitable place to stop.

"Children, I want you to stay here and rest. You can eat some bread and listen to the birds but do not come with us as it is too dangerous. We will go and collect fire wood so that we are warm tonight," said the mother and off they went.

Hansel and Gretel watched them go and ate their bread. After a while they tired of sitting and got up and wondered around in search of the birds that were singing. They lost track of time and did not realise that they had wondered far from the place they had been left.

They walked and walked and dark fell upon them.

"Hansel, I am scared," said Gretel. "We should have found our mother and father by now and be sitting safely by the warm fire at home."

"Never fear," said Hansel, "I am here and I will take care of you and when morning comes we will follow the sun which will lead us home."

They got very little sleep but eventually the sun started to rise and set off towards it. They had forgotten that the sun rises in the east and sets in the west and their home was in the west so they were walking away from their home. After many hours they were still in the thick forest and with sore feet Gretel said,

"Hansel are we close to home yet?"

"I cannot see," said Hansel, "but I do smell something nice and tasty". They followed the smell and then they saw the most wondrous sight. There was a little timber hut with a beautiful garden. There were rows and rows of big flowers that you could eat. There were strawberry coloured ones on chocolate coloured stems and marigolds galore. So hungry were Hansel and Gretel that they forgot about the stories that were told by the villagers about a wicked witch that lives in the forest and she eats children up.

"Do not go into the forest," they said, "for fear of your life."

Happily munching on the strawberry flowers with chocolate stems they did not notice this figure approaching them dressed in a black long flowing robe with a very pointy large brimmed hat. She gave them such a fright that they screamed.

"Don't be afraid," she said, "come on in, I have a lovely bowl of stew on the stove and you look hungry." Once inside she set bowls down on the table and from the large cauldron she scooped up the lovely smelling broth and placed two bowlfuls on the table for the children. Very soon, they were well fed and yawning. "Let me show you into the bedroom and you can have a sleep," said the woman dressed in black. Hansel and Gretel happily threw themselves on the soft beds and were quickly in a deep sleep.

Finally they woke but when Gretel went to open the door she found it would not open.

"Oh!" cried Gretel. "Hansel, do you remember what the older folk told us about the witch in the forest? Did you notice how she never smiles and always frowned? Did you see the black cat sitting on the window sill outside and what about that broomstick?. Do you think the stew were the other little children that came before us. Oh Hansel we cannot get out, what shall we do?" Hansel, calm as always, did not answer. He could see no way out but to panic would be pointless and he needed to concentrate.

"Gretel," he said, "when the wicked witch opens the door and comes to get us, I want you to stand behind the door on the chair and hit her on the head with this pillow. I will then grab her legs and tie her up and we will be free." With this plan in mind, the children waited quietly until they heard the witch coming down the corridor.

The door opened and there the lady stood with two bowls of ice cream. But, before she could say anything, Gretel had hit her with the pillow and Hansel had pushed her over to the floor. The lady fell, hurting her ankle and was in a great deal of pain.

"I only wanted to give you some ice cream before I take you to the edge of the forest and showed you the way to the village. Now I cannot walk."

Hansel and Gretel saw that the lady who never smiled was telling the truth and Hansel put on his thinking cap again. They were very sorry for what they had done and wanted to make amends.

"I know," he said, "I saw a hand cart outside, why don't you sit in it and then we can pull you whilst you show us the way."

"Yes," said the lady, "we can do that and maybe I will come into the village where the doctor can see to my ankle which is very painful."

It was the afternoon before they came to the edge of the forest. Hansel gave a huge sigh of relief because he could see his village now.

As the three of them walked along the main street towards the doctor, they saw a man mending a roof. He looked at the three of them and stared in disbelief. He scrambled down the ladder and ran towards them with open arms. The children wondered who this man was but, when they turned to look at the lady who was sitting in the cart, they saw that the lady had a beautiful smile and she looked radiant. The man came and scooped her up out of the cart and twirled her around and around.

"I thought I would never see you again!" he said. "When I was in Africa I was separated from my group and then I fell ill with a sleeping sickness. The local Masai tribe took me in but it was many months before I recovered and even more months before I could find my way home. When I did finally get back to the village, I was told you had left out of sorrow as you had been told I had died and no one knew where to find you".

"Oh" she said, "yes, I was so very sad when they told me. I did not want to see anyone anymore so I and my cat went into the forest where I stumbled across a woodcutter's cottage and there I made my home. I often sat and remembered the times we had together but I could not face people again. But now that you are here I can stay."

The two of them have never been separated since and the Hansel and Gretel did go home to their very worried parent who were so grateful that their two precious children had returned home safely.

The Delivery

Janet Findlay

Judy reached into her jean pocket for the five pounds. It was inside a sealed envelope that she'd been given the night before by the Nigerian woman in the detention centre.

Pausing at the entrance to the bleak tenement building, she took out the envelope, smoothed it flat and re-read the name and address scrawled on the front. Mr Ayodele Nnamani, 26/143 Railton Rd, Brixton, SE 5.

Not for the first time in the last 24 hours, she mentally rehearsed the message the woman had whispered to her as she handed her the envelope. "Tell my brother he must send a telegram to our parents in Lagos. To say I won't be on the plane. That I've been kept here for two days now and I don't know when I'll arrive there. But tell them not to worry about me and my son."

Judy closed her hand tightly around the envelope and cautiously began to walk into the building. It was unlike anything she'd ever seen before. Vast, dreary, neglected – imposing in a hopeless kind of way - as floor after floor concertina'd out above her. She paused on a first-floor landing.

There was a sudden shout from an upper balcony and she raised her eyes to see four black men staring down at her. They were silent as they watched her ascend the stairs, winding her way up and stopping on the next landing as she came closer to the fifth floor.

She cursed herself for feeling fearful. She was from New Zealand for heaven's sake. She'd never encountered racial hostility. But she didn't like the vibe from these men.

Her footsteps echoed eerily, a soundtrack to her racing thoughts. What the hell was she doing here? Not only in London, but in Brixton of all places! Acting like some do-gooding idiot, undertaking to carry a message from a stranger in a detention centre to a stranger in a ghetto. And a heavy-duty ghetto at that! And let's not even look at how she come to end up in a detention centre! She wasn't like the poor Nigerian woman arriving from Boston, who'd just innocently stood in the wrong queue with her fractious baby and been discriminated against by racist British immigration officials....

A large spray painted number five came into view on a wall to her left, defaced by all the usual graffiti. Well, she was on the right floor anyway. She'd arrived ... and she'd survived. The men on the other balcony seemed to have shifted away. Now all she had to do was find number 26 and Mr Ayodele Nnamani, then get the hell out of here.

She didn't have to search far. Number 26 was a doorway slightly to her right. She quickly ran her hands through her hair, straightened out her travel-worn denim jacket, took a deep breath and knocked. There was a movement in the curtains from a small window to the left of the door. A beat or two, and the door was cautiously pulled back.

An anxious looking black man, with a scar on his forehead, looked at her fearfully. He seemed to be a few years older than she. Mid-thirties. His eyes were full of pain.

"Hello," she began, her fingers clenching around the envelope with the five pound note in it. "I'm looking for... Ayodele Nnamani... Is that you? I've come –"

The man spoke quickly. "No, no, he is not here, he doesn't live here!" He began to close the door.

"Oh please!" Judy was starting to feel desperate at the thought of not delivering the envelope to somebody at least. "I have a message for him from his sister who I met at the Gatwick Airport detention centre yesterday ..."

"Who are you? Are you from the police?"

"No, no..." This was so difficult. "It's just that I promised her that when I got into London, I would deliver a message on her behalf. You see, she won't be able to let her parents know she's been detained, and they were going to travel in from the country to meet her plane in Lagos ... and ah, she's given me this for her brother to send her mother and father a telegram ..." Judy waved the envelope weakly in front of her as her voice trailed away. She should never have promised to do this.

"It is me." The man's eyes had lost their fear and his face had softened. "I am Ayodele. Please do come in!" He threw the door open then and stepped back politely to let her pass into the little hallway. Judy hesitated. The man smiled encouragingly and nodded. "Please, you are very kind." She took a step. And another. And then followed him into a large living room, furnished elaborately with bold paintings, and tall vases stuffed with feathers and artificial flowers. "Can I offer you coffee? Or would you prefer a sherry?"

Perched uncertainly on a burgundy velveteen sofa with a white lace antimacassar, Judy shook her head and stretched out her hand with the envelope. She had to make the delivery.

She took in yet another deep breath and said, almost as she'd rehearsed it, "Here is five pounds from your sister, to send your parents a telegram. She's been held at Gatwick for two days now, for no obvious reason, and she has no idea when she'll be released. Obviously, she won't be on the flight your parents planned to meet, but she wants them to know that she and her baby are safe."

Ayodeli Nnamani took the envelope from her and held it close to his chest like it contained much more than a five-pound note. Almost like it was precious.

There. It was done. The message had been delivered as promised.

On the flight back to Auckland, two days later, Judy found herself with ample time to reflect.

But was it going to be twenty-four hours of beating herself up for having been such an idiot? Imagining she could enter the UK on a $50 flight from New York ... with no return fare to New Zealand? Armed only with a mere intention - that of going on to Amsterdam to join an English-speaking theatre troupe, for who knows how long?

She opted instead for reflecting on her 'awfully big adventure'. Being treated as a wayward colonial by the British authorities, breakfasting on white bread, red jam, yellow cornflakes and black tea, sharing jokes with Pakistani over-stayers, hearing the stories of political refugees from South America, and sharing a room with a poor woman who'd simply joined the wrong queue because a baby's crying was doing her head in!

Judy remembered the scar on Ayodele's forehead. The result of a five-year old kid throwing a bottle at him at his first day at Medical School in England, he'd said. Arrgh! People!

But then there were people like her old friend Gretel, who'd responded immediately to her 'out of the blue' call from an airport detention centre and got her out on 'parole' for two days! Happily showing her the sights of London, and, somewhat against her better judgement, driving her to Brixton to fulfil a promise.

Actually, 24 hours in a plane can go quite fast providing you eat, drink and watch everything that's on offer. Which is what Judy did. And she found to her surprise that Smokey and the Bandit can stand up to three viewings. She liked Burt Reynolds and Sally Fields playing silly, reckless outsiders. Because when you're a globe-trotting free spirit of 30 going on 13, silly, reckless outsiders seem like your kind of people.

Knickers and Vicars

Carole Aveley

Why do we get embarrassed? Is it a fear of making a fool of ourselves? Whether it be slipping on a banana skin, or losing the power of speech at a vital moment or simply going to a party and finding the hostess is wearing an identical dress? The feeling is the same, we are overcome with shame because somehow we have been 'found wanting'. You could say caught on the wrong foot; maybe unprepared would describe the situation?

When we were very young these situations were particularly unbearable for we had no experience of how to deal with them. Slipping on a banana skin or falling down the stairs in front of others made us the focus of attention at a vulnerable moment. But that is not quite as bad as experiencing a complete loss of speech in public, is it? You might find yourself mumbling incoherent nonsense when you know perfectly well what you should be saying? That is certainly cause for blushing! As for turning up at a party to discover someone wearing that very same dress, which you had just purchased for next to nothing at the sales, is something quite unbearable until you actually 'grow up' and learn how to carry off such incidents.

So when we 'grow up' we gradually find that it happens less and less. It seems we learn to cope with these embarrassing situations, we develop a coping mechanism which clicks in and rescues us in the nick of time. Mostly.

I had a most devastating experience when a teenager - for a teenager, that is!

It was in the middle of a church service; we stood up for the hymn, kneeled down for a prayer, sat to listen to the lesson; when we stood up for the next hymn I felt my knickers sliding slowly downwards! I must explain here that they were rather large, black, school bloomers! We knelt for the next prayer and I wriggled a bit and managed to re-move them when we sat for the sermon. The people around me were very amused and I wanted to dig a hole and bury myself!

Compare this with an incident that happened to me twenty five years later. We were at a dance, and I was executing a rather energetic rock and roll move when - you've guessed it - my knickers started to slide!! This time they were itsy-bitsy red polka dot bikini panties! I gyrated a little more and they slid to the floor. I flounced out of them with an exaggerated twist and a grin – and my husband scooped them up triumphantly and popped them into his pocket - and we carried on dancing! You see there are advantages in growing older!

But I have learned to take more care of my knicker elastic!

Wednesday's Child

Carole Aveley

Well now, here's another little bundle of joy! But Wednesday's child is full of woe, and this one does not look too promising; she's a bit wimpy! I might have to give this one a helping hand to toughen her up.

She's going to be an only child I see, and the centre of her parent's attentions. That means she will develop into a selfish little being. Now I see her throwing temper tantrums and sulking when she can't get her own way. My goodness these sulks go on and on … and on!!!

Certainly, this is pretty weak and feeble material to work with, I wonder how I can turn her into something worthwhile?

Her father is now home from the war and decides to sign up with MI5 a branch of the Intelligence Service. He speaks German, French and Italian fluently, he accepts a tour of duty to post war Germany and takes his wife and child along for the ride. So my little bundle of sulky woe starts school at the English medium school for ex-pats, mostly service men's children.

A bit of bullying might give her some backbone! I'll see to that; children can be cruel, I'll lay it on thick. Now she's feeling sorry for herself, but she does have a friend, maybe there is a chance for her after all. She's not stupid, but is not absorbing much from this schooling – her arithmetic is abominable!! And, I'll share a secret with you, she is going to become a bookkeeper when she grows up!!! Father gets a transfer to Cologne, this will be the third junior school for our precious child.

Mother decides that her daughter should be doing better and returns to England with her to administer some serious extra tuition especially in arithmetic and enrols her in one of York's well respected junior schools in preparation for the 'eleven-plus' exams. Mother is determined that her child will go to grammar school. This is a bit daunting for our reluctant student. Father returns to England and they move to a little country pub, which necessitates another move, and another school, the fifth for our shy little girl, newcomers are viewed with suspicion, especially if they don't speak with a good old Yorkshire accent! The eleven-plus results enable her entry to the local grammar school – things are looking up. Father then achieves a job managing an hotel requiring another move and consequently her second senior school.

Father is full of adventurous spirit, he is restless in post war England, where rationing is still in force and life is dull and dreary, so he decides to leave England and go to Africa. His choice is Kenya. Mother is a bit reluctant because for her Africa is daunting, and Kenya even more so since the Mau-Mau rebellion is still being mopped up.

They embark on a liner in Southampton en route for Mombasa. The Bay of Biscay is its usual tempestuous self, tossing the ship around like a cork until they pass through the Straits of Gibraltar, entering the Mediterranean Sea. First stop Malta. They have a day ashore and eagerly explore the ancient stone city and battlements. This is exciting! Our young girl is now a teenager, making friends with a couple youngsters who live in Nairobi, where she will be going to boarding school. The ship sails serenely through the calm, blue Mediterranean to Port Said and into the Suez Canal. They are intrigued by the old Arabian buildings, the grand Mosques with graceful minarets are exotic! Tall palm trees appear occasionally in the desert on either side of them and Camels plod along the dunes bordering the Canal as they pass slowly by.

Quotes from the verses of Omar Kyhaam come to mind:
A book of verse, a jug of wine
and thou beside me
singing in the wilderness,
Ah wilderness were paradise ere now.

Next stop Aden on the very tip of Saudi Arabia – the ship stays out in the bay and rude boats row out to her with turbaned Arab curio sellers, dressed in white galabiyas who climb aboard spreading their wares on the decks; she buys a sandalwood carving of a camel. On shore bare, craggy mountains frame the town, no sign of any trees, just scruffy tin shanties. And it is Hot, like a furnace! Gosh this is a different experience!

They sail on rounding the Horn of Africa, then South to dock in Mombasa on the East coast. It is stiflingly hot and muggy! The town is depressingly scruffy; not an auspicious start to their anticipated new life. Coping with this torpid heat is tough, having just left a severe English winter.

They board a steam train which takes them into the interior through arid bushland for the twenty four hour journey to Nairobi. In the evening the bedding steward delivers two bed rolls and proceeds to make up the bunks – horror of horrors – a HUGE hunting spider crawls out of one and then scuttles back inside!! Yikes – her horrified screams convince the steward to remove the bedroll and replace it with a fresh one, which he kindly inspects and pronounces free of spiders!

Boarding school is the next hurdle to deal with in this journey towards making something out of this child. The New Girls Secondary School buildings are converted from ex-RAF billets, wooden shacks built up on stilts. Unfortunately this school is only temporary, it relocates up to Uganda, necessitating another change of schools. The Kenya High School (KHS) is a formidable fortress; three-story brick buildings forming a semi-circle. The windows have stout burglar bars, in the evening access to the dormitories is closed off with steel doors. The girls are taken to church in army lorries, with sturdy mesh instead of windows. These are the precautions that had to be taken during the Mau-Mau unrest. The school boys refer to the girls as heifers and the KHS as the heifer boma! [A boma is a stockade.]

Luckily our young lady attains her School Certificate, emerging like a butterfly from its chrysalis. I hope that I have built her into a resilient survivor; the role of 'Fairy Godmother' can be tough at times! I think I can now leave her to her own devices.

Shooting Time

Jenny Chriswick

Well, it's 4.00 am on Saturday and she has stirred. The birds are waking and you can clearly hear the Kookaburras saying good morning, get up it's a lovely day, and who ignores those very loud noises that sound like a Punch and Judy Show.

So it's the normal routine – bathroom, dress and grab a few dog treats to put in the pocket and out of the house. The horse is not too well at the moment, a bit old, being twenty seven, and now she is ill so she is in need of a little extra care. A walk to the shed and open up the big doors and that is the signal for the horse to walk painfully up to the feed bowl. It's heartbreaking to watch but hopefully the medications will start to kick in. The medication must be upsetting the horse because nothing will tempt her to eat. However, yesterday the familiar food, although not the best to be giving to a sick horse, was devoured. Not sure if it was the food or the fact that a certain person was standing and watching every mouthful and the horse was too frightened not to eat.

Satisfied that the horse is comfortable and eating, it's time for the morning walk in the paddock. It's a twenty acre paddock, heavily treed, which seems to always be dropping limbs or, worse still, falling over so it's a matter of doing a bit of maintenance whilst walking and checking fences. The morning walk is usually five kilometres. The dogs, three, enjoy these walks and are continually checking up every tree and down every hole for smells of wildlife and what they have been up to overnight. Sometimes a rabbit has ventured onto the property and off go the dogs in a fruitless pursuit of what might be at the end of the scent. This means she does five kilometres and they do ten. Those are good mornings because then they sleep all day whilst she gets on with work or other things that need to be done. This morning, as it is quite warm, there is chance of a quick swim in the dam. May be not this morning though as she seems determined to bypass the dam and get back to the house.

Well, normally its breakfast at this time but not today. I see that she is packing a blue bag and yes, there is the special coat going in. On go the dog harnesses and they are bundled into the car and carefully attached to the safety leads. In goes the esky and the 'blue bag' with the special coat and even though it's only 5.30 the car is reversed and we are off.

The dogs quickly settle as there is a long drive in front of everyone, at least an hour. The radio is on, the roads are empty and its beautiful scenery and clear blue skies as they drive up the Brisbane Valley Highway, over the Wivenhoe Dam wall and up the road towards Esk, a little country town 100 kilometres from Brisbane.

Finally, Esk, and turn the corner and there are her friends, other silly people who get up at the crack of dawn. Now there is a convoy as they set off down the road, turning left and right and finally they are on a dirt track in the middle of who knows where but finally everyone stops. They all get out and there is a lot of pointing and walking around this beautiful, large cattle property.

The catapults – or throwers as they are often called – and guns are taken out of the car and carried some distance. Again, there is a lot of pointing and measuring and the walky-talkies are now being used to communicate with those people on the throwers whilst the others are staying by the white starting pegs.

That done, it's … no wait, it's time for a coffee. Everyone comes back to where the cars – or I should say utes – are and they gather around on their camping chairs. Outcome the coffee flasks and a few biscuits. It's a catch-up on who's done what, doing what and what will be tried this morning. There is no rush. It's a lovely morning and here they are sitting by the edge of rather large dam built for cattle in the middle of nowhere with not a car to be heard, or a bird for that matter. There are few cattle in the far distance who don't seem at all interested in their intruders and carry on eating and chewing the very long, brown grass.

Well, finally, everything is gathered up and put away. Two people walk up to the catapults in the distance. Another stands by the first set of white pegs and someone else is standing between them with a gun and large clipboard.

She comes back to the car which means that I can get out now. I have been sitting for so long so I need to stretch my legs for a minute and then we walk towards the white starting pegs. She stops, talks to the lady on the left who hands her a gun. This is the hilarious part; she is not "into" guns at all and even opening them to load needs an instruction pack. On previous occasions she has discharged when the barrel is pointing at her foot so it's really good that they only give her blank cartridges.

This gundog retrieving business is fun; it's a mock shoot but no live animals or shot is used. Some of the people do go out to the properties and shoot rabbits and pretend they are in the 18th century shooting for their evening tucker. They never say if they actually do shoot the rabbit or miss every time. It's always just "they went shooting".

Ok, she has the gun and is now walking toward the second set of pegs. She stops, closes the barrel, I look at her, then she lifts the gun and shoots and then I see it, it's a plastic duck flying through the air a hundred metres away, having been launched from the throwers that were positioned earlier. "Fetch" she says and off I run, down the hill and into the distance to pick up the plastic duck. I am after all, her much loved retrieving dog and this is what I love doing.

The Far Flung Pan

Philip J Bradbury

My little six-year-old mind didn't understand what the yelling was about but my eyes could see my father turning red, thumping the dining table and yelling ferociously, belligerently. They could also see my mother's pleading cries, her bowed head, her sad eyes. Stuck in the middle, I forced my body to stay as still as it could. I even tried to stop breathing and probably did for long moments. I tried to pretend I wasn't there so they wouldn't notice and turn on me.

"Oh, John, why can't we just have ..." beseeched my mother, till she was interrupted.

"Because I bloody well said so and that's it!" said my father, his voice going quiet and icy as he stormed out. I heard him thumping round in the porch, putting his boots on and then stamping out to the dog kennels. I dared look up for a second and saw him storming off with five dogs trotting behind him, all happy to be out of their kennels; their smiles at odds with my father's thundering scowl.

"It's okay, Philip, you're okay," said Mum, trying to reassure me as she wiped her eyes. I wanted to help her and wanted to run at the same time. I waited. She sat, alternately staring out the window and smiling wanly at me. I didn't move, not wanting to do the wrong thing, whatever that was.

Life, as we know, abhors a vacuum. When gentle, tiny sorrow leaves a room, her wild, bumptious brothers, rage and vengeance crash in to fill the space. After what seemed a lifetime – in my little life – she suddenly looked up, squared her chin and muttered something about getting him back one day.

"Come on, no point moping," she said, standing up. "Let's get the jobs done and we'll have our own fun, shall we."

"Okay," I said, unsure of what fun she meant in this most un-fun moment.

We cleared the table, stacked the dishes, ready to wash them and she suddenly announced that she needed to get outside for some air. I thought there was air in the house but what did I know. We fed the chooks, collected the eggs, watered the vegetable garden, picked peas and carrots and pottered about outside till she decided she'd had enough air. Time to finish the dishes. By now, Dad must have been gone for a couple of hours and I was still uneasy. She seemed to have forgotten the fight but I hadn't and feared he'd return any moment to escalate it. However, I dried the dishes she was washing and put them away.

Then I heard his footsteps.

"Is that Dad?" I asked, ready to run.

"He's early for morning tea but it must be him," she said, looking at me, puzzled. His routine was legend and he seldom varied it.

"Perhaps he wants to say sorry," I ventured, hopefully.

"Sorry?" she demanded. "I'll give him sorry!" By now she was on the last of the dishes; the large roasting pan. She scooped the pan full of cold, dirty, fatty water and stood there, braced. She timed her performance to the split second and waited with the heavy, grease and water-filled pan weighing heavily in her arms. At the precise moment that we imagined he'd be reaching for the door knob, she lunged.

Mum swung the door open and let him have it. The pan slipped and so he got the rancid water and a pan on the head.

"There, that'll serve you right …" she said, training off.

"Well, that's a nice welcome, Mrs Bradbury," said a strange voice. I had to see who it was, looked around and saw Lionel, the local stock agent, standing there, with a smile, dripping clothes and a pan at his feet while he rubbed his sore head.

At that moment Dad appeared and he stopped and frowned. Then he summed it up and laughed the loudest I'd ever heard him laugh. The other two soon joined in and then I did as relief flooded over me.

As far as I knew, that day's argument wasn't resolved. It was simply heaped onto the growing pile of resentments to be used as fuel for next week's argument. However, the story of The Far Flung Pan is talked about far and wide and is still whispered to children in dark moments to raise a smile, to warn of rages of sin and to look before you leap.

The Shrinking Dress

Judy de la Mare

I love shopping though I wouldn't call myself a shopaholic. That is I am not addicted to it, but enjoy more the browsing aspect. I like to imagine how a certain item would look at home without the need to actually purchase it.

I also like to try on clothes. Again just to see if a blouse suits or a dress flatters. Thus I was at the local shopping centre with my youngest daughter about twenty years ago when we saw a striking medieval style dress in a shop window. The dress was fitted on a mannequin and looked amazing. It was a deep green with embroidered panels and a fitted bodice. Would it look so good on me?

While my daughter looked around the shop I asked the assistant if they had one in my size. Anticipating a sale she searched out the back and returned with that perfect dress. Taking it into the fitting room I was surprised that it didn't have a zipper, but carefully eased it over my head and stood back to view the result in the mirror. Not bad. I called to my daughter for a second opinion and she agreed that it suited me. I hadn't set out on this trip to buy anything at all and was now debating with myself as to whether I could justify the expense of this dress.

Starting to remove it, I then realised that this was not going to be easy. Something that had slipped on so readily was a problem to get out of. It somehow had moulded itself to my body and every time I raised my arms the dress hugged me more tightly.

I am claustrophobic at the best of times. Now the dressing room seemed to shrink with the dress whilst I was expanding. It must have been a nervous reaction but I was puffing up like a toadfish. I really thought that the dress would need to be cut off me. How embarrassing that would be! I could imagine the staff living off that funny story for years.

Desperately I called to my daughter. Now with both of us in the dressing room there was even less space for such a tricky operation. However she slowly calmed me down and with much struggling I was released from that horrid, horrid dress. A most embarrassing moment was averted.

Chickens

Paul Howlett.

Chickens are birds that lay eggs. The number of chicken eggs that I have eaten would fill a normal household room by now. Here are a number of chicken and egg stories that have caused mirth and destruction.

The first chicken egg story was a funny film clip from an early Dad and Dave movie. The local priest was visiting Dad and Dave's family, then Dave brought out an egg and dropped it on the ground in front of everyone, and of course, the egg broke releasing a bad odour that stank to high heaven. Everyone around held their nose and moved away from the egg, and the final laugh was the dog removing itself from the vicinity.

My second egg story was one of childhood memories. When my brother Bruce and I visited my uncle's home for Christmas Holidays we were fascinated by our uncle's extensive chicken runs, housing and pens. Next to one of the chicken pens was a bench and on the bench were a number of eggs just sitting in the sun. My brother poked one of the eggs with his finger and it exploded. I managed to duck and miss getting covered in rotten smelly egg yolk, but my poor brother was not so fortunate. He copped the lot and it put him off eating eggs for years.

When I was a child we kept half a dozen chickens in the back yard for the eggs, and we also ate the chickens. Well - we ate only a few chickens when my mother declared it was not worth the hassle of plucking and cleaning the chicken. So that ended our home bred, killed, plucked and cooked chicken dinners.

Now, of course, we look to buy our chickens from the shop. I see people taking cooked chooks to the checkout every time I shop at the supermarket. Normally when I walk past the hot cooked chicken display I see that most of the product has been sold. I like eating chicken but I cook them myself and I always cook the free range frozen chickens. The cheaper frozen chickens are loaded with too much fatty bulky flesh.

Chickens produce eggs – caged eggs, free range eggs, organic eggs and I think that the branding of free range eggs together with organic eggs is an excuse to double or triple the price in the supermarket. Supermarkets claim to have fresh produce, but when I bought a dozen eggs off a fellow student from Toowoomba, I knew what fresh eggs were really like. They were tasty, colourful and really fresh with natural thinner shells.

One of my early childhood endeavours with chickens came to a sudden end after my mother found me chasing the chickens with a pair of scissors. My intention was to cut off some lovely chicken tail feathers for myself. My mother showed me the error of my ways and I was never allowed to run about carrying scissors ever again! I never obtained any tail feathers.

This brings me to the subject of chicken feathers. When you look at the hats of old army men, you can see that they were adorned with a number of lovely tail feathers from various kinds of chickens. Ladies too, had many different hats adorned with chicken feathers but now all that is out of fashion. That is a little sad as hats with lots of feathers in days gone by always had a touch of fashion eloquence.

The Game

Janet Findlay

"Chickens!" Al exclaimed, as he slapped six scrabble tiles down on the old wooden table. My friend Vicky and I exchanged glances, and turned to look at him with amusement.

It was a beautiful afternoon in early spring. We were sitting outside on the deck of his little cottage at Mt Maroon, playing what we referred to as The Game.

"What do you mean 'chickens'?" I said to him. "You've just spelt 'bounty'!"

"Yes, yes…but don't you remember chickens? Twenty chickens?"

"I've no idea what you're talking about.." Vicky gave him a wary smile.

I held my breath. I hoped this wouldn't put her off. I'd only recently introduced her to Al and I hadn't told her that he was sometimes known as Weird Al. After Weird Al Yankovich, of course..

"Oh, I remember now," I interjected. I had a feeling this wasn't going to proceed well. I rearranged my word tiles in neat lines in front of me. "He's – um - probably talking about Hillary 'Twenty Chickens' Clinton but we don't need to go…"

"What?" Vicky was looking distinctly puzzled now. Across the table from her, Al doubled over, cackling with laughter - while at the same time managing to run his eyes over my tiles. He was looking to pilfer my words, the rat! Oh well, it's all part of the Game. (By the way, it's not regular scrabble we're talking about here. It's a variation called Racing Scrabble. But today, it's dragging a bit, because Vicky's a new recruit.)

"Hillary 'Twenty Chickens' Clinton!" Al repeated chuckling, as he reached over and removed my perfectly good word EASE and, with a bit of re-shuffling, transformed it into the word MEASLES.

"Good one," I murmured with grudging approval. I noticed Vicky was frowning slightly.

I shouldn't really have had any expectation that she and Al might hit it off. Not two loners in their early sixties. How unrealistic am I? Besides, just because I knew that Vicky liked intellectual men, didn't mean to say that intellectual men liked intellectual women. In fact, quite the reverse has been true in my experience.

"Come on you two," Vicky sounded a little peeved. "What's with this 20 chickens/Hillary Clinton thing?"

I looked at Al, he was still giggling helplessly. I could see I'd have to provide the explanation.

"OK. Well, it's not a nice story," I said. "It's one that Al got from his online conspiracy theory mates…but apparently, in some Middle Eastern country - I can't remember which - is it Libya – there's a bounty on Hillary Clinton's head…and the bounty is…

"20 chickens!" I could see that Al just loved saying it. This wasn't going well.

"Oh, my god!" Vicky looked appalled. "That's ghastly!"

"Yep, insane, isn't it?" I shot a glance across at Al who was wordlessly thumping his hand on the table with an expression of - what was that - surely not …glee? Better to plough on and get this whole horrible tale over with. "Yes, if someone… um… does that, they'll be – ah, rewarded with 20 chickens!"

"Twenty chickens!" Al crowed, slapping the table harder this time. The tiles jumped and jived. He really was a bit mad. Too much time spent with his cyber mates and not enough time in live human company - which can sometimes exert a moderating effect. Sometimes. "That's all they think she's worth!" he positively shouted.

"So….you're obviously not a Hillary Clinton fan…." Vicky began.

"Not a Hillary Clinton fan! Hah! That's the understatement of the century!" Al swung his chair around closer to hers, preparing to give her the full benefit of his complex political stance. In detail.

Mentally, I threw in the towel. Vicky, whom I'd assessed to be a gentle soul, would surely hate his extreme views. And if he didn't alarm her with his radicalism, he'd certainly bore her to tears with his long-winded exposition of it. I tried to switch off from the intense diatribe - from which words like Warmonger and Murderer were frequently springing...Instead, I tried to focus on our sets of words, looking to see what I could beg, borrow or steal. Because that's all part of the Game.

Ah ha! I saw my chance to change Al's measles into teased and I did it. It was my turn, I reasoned. Then I looked at Vicky's words and contemplated changing date into mated. But that would be a bit low... To score points from someone who was new to the game - especially when they weren't looking. I felt ashamed of myself for even considering it. Of course, on the scale of lowness, it wasn't in the same league as a twenty-chicken bounty on Hillary Clinton's life! But still...

"It's - ah - a beautiful spot here, isn't it?" Vicky said too loudly, jerking her chair back from the table. The sudden movement made a grating noise. I could understand why she was so keen to change the subject.

"Ah yes, I love it!" Al was sounding particularly genial and expansive after having 'chewed her ear' for a good five minutes. He leaned back in his swivel chair. "I always like to say if you're going to be marooned anywhere, there's no better place in the world for it than Mt Maroon!" Vicky laughed - a bit more than the joke warranted, I thought. Doubtless with relief.

Al took a slug from his bottle of beer which had been unattended for an unusually long time, and we all looked around appreciatively at the view from the deck.

As I said, it was a late afternoon in spring. It hadn't started to get really hot yet. The silhouette of the mountain was clear and sharp. The three yellow and pink frangipani trees at the fence line were opening into flower. I caught a waft of their fragrance. It was intoxicating.

Al drained his beer. "Well, back to The Game!" he declared. "Are you two okay for drinks?"

Vicky still had some of Al's 'secret recipe' lemon squash in a tall glass. "Yes, I'm fine." she murmured.

"Yep, I'm good," I said smartly, taking a sip of my cold coffee. The sooner we finished the game, the sooner I could extricate Vicky from this social train wreck, and head off back to Ipswich.

"Ah ha! Who's been playing with my words?" Al was on the ball. "What happened to my Measles?"

"I'd been planning that one for a while," I protested, "and then I turned up a D! What's a girl to do?"

Al laughed good-naturedly. His eyes scanned the assortment of our upturned tiles.

"Oh, do excuse me, ma'am," he said in a gallant tone to Vicky, as he reached across her and swiftly picked out some tiles from her small collection. He rapidly rearranged them and added them to his pile. The bugger. He'd done it. Converted DATE into MATED.

"Oh, I was going to do that," I groaned.

"Too late!" Al rubbed his hands together. He was winning. "Coming up to End Game now!"

"Just remember it can all change in the last few minutes!" I warned him. And it's true. The Game is not always predictable.

And nor was it today. Fired up by impending defeat, I changed Al's word wench into quench. On a roll, I turned Vicky's word Cute into Elocute. But what made it a draw, was when Al went into overdrive and somehow combined Elocute and quench into Eloquent. I can't remember how now. But it was the last word of the Game.

As we came to say our goodbyes, I was surprised at how solicitous Al was when he handed Vicky the soft pashmina shawl she'd left draped over a chair. I was even more surprised when Vicky reached out and gave Al a lingering hug. And you could have knocked me over with a feather when I heard her say - quite flirtatiously, "You know, there's nothing I admire more in a man than ... Eloquence!"

The Magic Faraway Tree

Judy de la Mare

The weather was perfect – a bright blue sky dotted with a few fluffy white clouds, a gentle breeze and not too hot and not too cold. Jo, Bessie and Fanny were sitting in the shade of the huge old tree and talking about the shapes that they could see in the clouds. Jo saw a rabbit, Bessie a flower and Fanny a bird. It was a lovely way to spend their time. Then Bessie noticed a small door at the base of the tree. The three friends decided to investigate and climbing higher they discovered some arched windows. Peeking through the glass their eyes met an Angry Pixie – the window was opened and cold water was poured on their heads. "How rude" they said to each other.

Climbing higher they came to another door. Inside this house they could hear loud snoring. It was Mr. Watzisname, and they thought it best not to disturb him.

At the top of the tree the branches disappeared into the fluffy white clouds and it was here that they found the entrance to the Magical Lands. They could leave their world behind and move into other special places. Moon-face, the man who lived below in the round house told them that they must explore quickly and then return or they would be stuck in that place forever.

Boldly they went on their first adventure. Stepping into the cloud they were met with a vast expanse of yellow sand. It was a desert – there were large spiky plants which hurt them when touched, and it was so very hot with nowhere to sit in the shade. They didn't like this place and ran back to the tree.

The next day they worked up the courage to try again. They climbed the great tree full of funny little houses and stepped off again into the clouds. Now before them were enormous, white mountains covered with snow. It was much prettier than the desert but so cold. They began to shiver and thought that they really didn't like it much more than the desert. They ran back to the tree and met Moon-face. He had a slippery dip in his house which he let them use to get quickly to the bottom of the tree where they could get warm.

A week went by and the three friends thought that they would try the magical lands once more. On their third ascent they decided that if this time the land was indeed not magical then there would be no more expeditions. So it was with some trepidation that they stepped onto the cloud. This time they saw giant trees even larger than the faraway tree, covered in lush green foliage. The noise of screaming colourful birds was deafening as was the roar of a massive river below. It was a tropical rainforest and Jo, Bessie and Fanny felt right at home. For the 3 little marmoset monkeys from the zoo, this was heaven. They had returned to their natural home and this time there would be no returning. The Magical Faraway tree had delivered their dream.

Shorts

Carole Aveley

Australian women in short shorts
Neat, trim, flashy;
I envy their long slim legs.
Sassy!

Suddenly denim was all the rage
Even torn and mucky,
With ragged hems.
Scruffy!

But the latest trend
Is lacey trimming
With cheeks a-peeping.
Riveting!

Chicken Soup

Carole Aveley

*C*hicken Soup for the Soul is a book of short inspirational true stories and motivational essays about ordinary people's lives. It was first printed in 1993.

I came across it not long after my husband passed away, and I found solace in many of its brief uplifting stories.

I have today had a look on the internet and discovered that there are 250 books in the Chicken Soup for the Soul series!!! That is crazy! I don't object to anyone making money – if the demand is there, but isn't this a bit over the top?

Some titles I saw are: Chicken Soup for the Cancer Survivor's Soul; Chicken Soup for the Divorce and Recovery soul; Chicken Soup for the Dog Lover's Soul … Mother's Soul, Father's Soul, Teacher's Soul, Chicken Soup for the Bride, for the Golfer and even – the Scrap booker's Soul! Can you believe it?

I searched some more and eventually found it – Chicken Soup for the Soul Cookbook!

Oh, well, the authors Jack Canfield and Mark Victor Hansen, have obviously got onto a good thing. I discovered that they sold out the company in 2008, after fifteen years of extremely successful marketing. I expect they are both millionaires now. Good for them.

One must give credit where it's due. Jack Canfield's Chicken Soup came into my life just when I needed it and I am grateful to him. When he dies, I hope his ability and success is recognized and the obituary is eloquent.

Give Me Time

Jenny Chriswick

'Chicken' we would call our friends if they would not take on a challenge or they were scared of surroundings. "Don't be a chicken," we would say. "Be brave."

I could see my husband struggling with a decision he had to make. That same look was on his face as when he was being called chicken or faint hearted. The look of anguish made my heart melt. Here was my true love, my soul mate, the person to whom I had never had to say sorry, no explanations needed. I could be "just me".

I wanted to tell him I loved him but I could not. I wanted to touch him but I could not. I wanted him to tell me the problem but I could not ask.

I could just lay there, a body on a bed surrounded by monitors which beeped. I could still see my husband but I had no way of communicating. Something had switched off in my brain; I know that, but something had remained too. Why did he not hear my silent words, not see the look behind my blank eyes? I was here.

What was all this tubing down my throat and puffing air into my lungs? If only they would take it out, I could show them that I could breathe. I would get better. I would need to work hard, yes. Baby steps, a little each day. I would teach my brain to reconnect, to grow new neurotransmitters. I know I could do it so why all the frowns and sad faces around my bedside. Why the tears from my loved ones. There is no need to worry, I am fine, just a little disconnected. I am just like a computer, missing a wire here and there. So why doesn't someone fix it?

Its night time and much quieter now. Less hustle and bustle. It's just me, my husband and these noisy machines. He is holding my hand, stroking it and crying.

"It is just a matter of time," I am saying to him, "all I need is a little time so no need to be so sad. I am strong, I can do this."

We had survived so much in our years together. Looking back, the problems seem trivial now but then they seemed like insurmountable hurdles. We were like the roly poly dolls we had as children which you could never knock over. We would poke them and over they would go and bounce straight up. That's life though. A constant stream of challenges and you either succumb or conquer. Together we conquered when it mattered and grew from the experience. We spread our wings. Nothing was going to stop us doing anything we cared to do. We could do anything if we put our minds to it.

So why can't I tell him this is just one more hurdle. Why does he not tell me this is just one more hurdle and this is the plan forward? Why does he just sit at my bedside and do nothing but look sad and cry and stroke my hand. I can feel it and it's lovely.

Morning is here and my husband has slumped in the chair and is sleeping awkwardly. The nurse comes in and checks this tube and that switch and this bag and straightens the bed clothes. He is awakened by this activity but he looks as if had not slept. So drawn and haggard. He looks a lost soul and I want to put my arms around him and tell him I will take care of him, just give me time.

The doctors come in. They're not looking glum. They listen to my lungs and heart, they read the charts. They put something on my head and a yet another machine starts to whir and spit out paper with lots of not so squiggly lines. They all go outside including my husband and I am left alone again with the machines. It's a surreal feeling, like an out of body experience. I feel like I am in the room but nobody can see me.

Only my husband returns. He seems less anguished now, more at peace. He comes to the bedside again and takes my hand and kisses my forehead. He sits down and looks at my face.

He is reminiscing on some of wonderful times we had and how much love we had shared and how lucky we had been to have had good health and be able to take all the glorious opportunities that had unfold-ed before us. Then he talked on how we had discussed organ donation and how we would love to help someone else when our time comes.

How it would feel that we lived on in some good person who was happier for having a new heart or anything of ours that still worked.

But wait, why are we talking on this topic? Now is not the time. We should be talking about the plan of work so that I can fix my brain. Why can I not move my hand he is stroking? Why can he not hear me?

The doctors come back in and my husband nods to them. Slowly the machines are turned off. As my breathing slowly ceases, my husband sits by the bedside holding my hand and talks of the wonderful love he has for me with such eloquence.

Have You Never ...

Jenny Chriswick

I thought that the senior moments were getting more as I became older but, on reflection, it seems they have always been around but, when younger, we called them embarrassing moments.

I mean, have you never walked around proudly in your new tee shirt displaying the long strip of Sellotape displaying in large numbers the size down the back. Or put it on back to front and thought you were setting a fashion trend.

Or pressed redial and started on a long dialogue about last night's date with all the intimate detail to find out, when the recipient is allowed to get a word in, it's your father on the end of the line and not your best friend.

Gosh, emails get me every time. Christmas is that time when one tends to repeat oneself when sending ecards or those now infamous Christmas letters. Have you never copied and pasted and left in content that that person was never meant to see or for that matter pressed "reply all" instead of reply and told the whole world how you have "feelings" towards a certain person.

I can't believe you have never signed the draft email to the boss "love and kisses" and accidentally sent it before re- editing.

I found the "insert pictures" button one day on this scheduling programme I was using and was having some fun with the current plan we had in place for this particularly ambitious project, just practising as one does. However, I don't think the boss was impressed when he passed my desk and saw that I had put the "dig a massive hole to the other side of the world" cartoon on the earthworks portion of the schedule and King Midas counting his gold sovereigns cartoon at the end of the schedule, not to mention the "Hah Hah just wish" written across another portion.

Open plan offices should be banned. How many times do people walk up behind you or stand at your side staring at your computer screen and there you are furiously trying to explain that you are 'on the first pass of this draft" and assuring them that the final proof will have more eloquent language befitting the professional standard of the office?

Have you never had a Nanna nap in a meeting and given an answer that was totally irrelevant to the question and then tried to back pedal or, worse, get completely tongue tied.

Sometimes it's not only offices that look the same. Sometimes each day seems the same. Have you never turned up to work on Sunday thinking its Monday and wonder why no one else is there.

Have you never tried to unlock the wrong car, swearing this is your car but you actually parked on the floor below? And it's even worse when it's a hotel room you are trying to enter and you are on the wrong floor.

Frequent flying has its issues too. Imagine boarding the plane with last weeks' boarding pass. One should never use your boarding pass as a page marker. Then, when the correct one is found and you are seated, a rather large person is looking down at you demanding that you vacate this seat numbered 69 immediately as it is his. Then walk your way to number 96 with head held high.

I walked off the plane, one very early morning, in my work boots that were only four years old but I thought the ground felt a little warm and soft but put it down to jetlag. The lower layer of my rubber soles were left on the tarmac as I walked. The consumable age it is called as the glue had passed its expiry date and no longer held the rubber soles to the boot..

Then I was standing in the international airport departure queue one morning, having taken only one day off work, and I look across to the adjacent queue and straight into the eyes of my boss. Try saying "everyone flies to Australia for a day and No, I am not going for a job interview" convincingly.

Sunday night is laundry night when working away and I was staying in a rather posh five-star hotel and, of course, the laundromat is in the basement. No problem, I can use the stairs and no one will see me in my … aah … let us say casual gear. Laundry done and I walk up the stairs and tug at the door handle. They are one-way locks – you can get off the floor but not on the floor. Ok, not the end of the world so down the stairs it is, through the endless tunnels of the basement and finally a door which leads to the STREET! Still Ok, a short walk around the building but then I hear talking and shouting and assume it's the local gangs and this is not a safe place to be. I run through the carpark, laundry in my arms, and arrive at the foyer totally breathless and flustered. "Just walk as if this is a normal event," I am saying to myself as I re arrange the ironed clothes on hangers that are over my fingers. "Everyone dresses this way and carries their laundry on Sunday and then has to stand for five minutes in a five-star hotel foyer whilst all the lifts seem to be on the 25th floor for ever."

However, when one is in a mining camp the laundry is done for you. All you have to do is put the laundry in a bag with your room number on it and, hey presto, the next day it's back, fully laundered. Walking through the office, large open plan as usual, I hear the deep voice of the senior supervisor yelling across the whole floor, "Jenny, your knickers don't fit me!" Immediate panic. Which ones did I wear yesterday?

I swear I am too old to run for trains but, sometimes, you must as these days you never know when the next one will come. But then it takes half an hour to get your breath back and you pretend these are the new deep breathing exercises you learnt at yoga classes.

Trains are so crowded in peak hour that one finds oneself closer to strangers than you would your significant other. How many times are you standing back to back, sometimes front to back and sometimes front to front, and wondered what is that sticking in me and tried to pretend that it's nothing.

Worst still, you think you have plugged in the head phones to your new iphone and stand listening to a tape which is going on about, deep breath, sink lower, imagine you are on a cloud and on and on. Then you realise they are only half in and everyone is having to enjoy this meditation tape.

Oh the safety of home where nothing is embarrassing, it's just normal.

The Impromptu Exercise

Everyone was given 2 minutes to write - on one piece of paper - the start of a story and - on another - the ending. These pieces of paper were shuffled and everyone took an ending and a beginning, ensuring they didn't take their own. They then had five minutes to write the story between their randomly chosen beginning and end. The italicised words are the ones we were given to start with.

Was The nightmare Over?

Jenny Chriswick

He emerged from the woods, blood dripping from the wound in his hand. Who had shot him, he did not know, but he was sure he was going to find out and get his revenge.

Now, without the element of surprise working against him, he armed himself with rifles and hand pistols and carefully retraced his steps back into the wood. It was easy to find the trail left behind by the attacker as he had been a tracker, taught by Navaho Indians. It wasn't long before he came to the end of the trail and found not one offender but ten offenders, all surprised at his arrival but prepared to defend themselves.

An almighty cacophony of shots was heard and finally it was silent.

Was the nightmare over? Could I be sure? Whatever the outcome, I was finished.

How On Earth?

Paul Howlett

How on Earth did I arrive at this point in my life? And in this place?
It was bizarre. My family disowned me, my head is all over the place and yet, because of the strong choices I had made, there I was at the top of the mountain of difficulties with my physique intact, my home life a dream come true ...

There had never been a better time!

Valley Of The Nile

Carole Aveley

Come join me on this journey through the Valley of the Nile.
It is hot, humid and we are sticky with sweat. We board a feluka which takes us up river as far as the Aswan Dam. From here we will walk – the aim is to reach the Valley of the Kings.

Tom strides ahead, confidently following the guide but then he slips and misses his footing. *Tumbling down a crevass, he is bitten by a snake on the ankle. His eyes closed and he breathed his last breath.*

The Missing Phone

Mark Grieveson

When she got to work she realised she had left her mobile phone on the kitchen table. There was insufficient time to go back. This created a sense of disquiet which permeated her whole day. She struggled through the morning and breathed a sigh of relief when the lunch hour arrived.

She went to the corner pub, ate a sausage roll, downed two glasses of white wine and a Valium.

She floated through the afternoon as if on autopilot and carefully drove home. As she slammed the door shut she exclaimed, "Thank Christ that's over!"

Lions Roar

Philip J Bradbury

When lions roar at day break is the time my heart stops. I pause, knowing I must rise, meet the day and take charge of the platoon, the platoon of equally frightened young men.

The Boers were ferocious and unremitting and, though the war's over long ago, the fear of yet another day of blood and screams still fills my ears and thumping chest.

Yes, Africa's not for sissies!

Skin Colour

NK

I had a farm in Africa with several dogs and native helpers. I'd always enjoyed being out in the bush with my dogs, especially in the early mornings. And, as I rambled I often came across my native helpers, tending their gardens before their days work for me began.

One day I heard them talking about how it must feel to have white skin. It had never occurred to me to think about it before but I realised quickly what a difference skin colour could make.

If only I'd known how others thought before this story began.

I Need Not Permission

Philip J Bradbury

I need not permission to love this sweet land
When soft beckons nostalgia, her kindly open hands
I remember a thousand years, then a thousand thousand more
Reaching for pebbles on any any shore
The large tale is told, breathed from these stones
The old story comes quiet, from deep our naked bones
Buried quiet in forgotten places, a whisper away
Is our legacy, destiny and fleeting eternal each day
The creator, our oneness, our source, spared nought
For us was this created, moulded, lovingly wrought
Hir[2] tears were shed and the oceans were full
Garrigarrang[3], the vast ocean highway, to which we're pulled
Hir breath expelled, our air, lightness of life
Burra[4] our in-breathing, our release from all strife
Hir flesh then shed, in a trice, gladly given all
Bamal[5], our mother, a safe place to fall

I need not permission to love this sweet fable
It is me, it is you, it sings us movingly stable
Onto her body, exquisitely strewn, texture and hue
Was given, her garments, pristine, gentle and new
Hir heavy green coat thrown down, upsprung tall trees
Anchored the earth, enriching the air, hoping to please
Her light skirt released, floated, hung delicately, alighted
The grasslands were spread, green and brown delighted

2	Hir denotes him or her
3	Garrigarrang is Aboriginal for the sea
4	Burra is Aboriginal for the sky
5	Bamal is Aboriginal for the earth

To keep these fine garments in fine flowing style
She pondered a moment, an aeon, a fairly long while
You see, buttons and laces do serve us a reason
For form, for grace and movement each season
Then thought, desire and intention begat form
For that is how the animals were gracefully born
The bison, hippo, tiger and bear, donkey and goat
From the buttons of this magnificent coat

I need not permission to love varied creations
Diverse skins, sounds, behaviour and hilarious machinations
Then snake, lizard, spider, cockroach and all
From zips, pins and fasteners they coyly did fall
Some swam through her tears, some plodded the ground
While others flew, glided on breath, enough to go round
For a moment, an aeon, a fairly long time
Was there balance, acceptance, sublimely all rhyme
Till one fine day when the sun did shine
Someone wanted more, not yours, it's mine
The fear spread in miraculous rapid degree
And soon was ripped buttons and coat, creature and tree
The timid illusion of lack, like a blazing fire spread
Till not only creator, but vast minds were dead

For a moment, an aeon, a fairly short time
My permission not granted, ground out as grime
Of unity and oneness was there nothing but proof
Till fear took hold and sanctified new truth
Not enough time, not enough stuff, all of these fade
If it's yours, not mine, I'm doomed, a story was made
The creator gave all, their finest their last
Till we turned grateful about, expired it so fast
Are there more rips than coat, beyond repair?
The skirt ground dust, too threadbare and sheer?
Are the buttons and catches too few to recall?
Can the rent garments be sewn back at all?
I need not permission to plead the why oh why
For dawning the end, exhausts my last cry

Chooks, Bikes and Cars

Philip J Bradbury

Chickens they all call them now. You know, those dumb and clucky, head bobbing, egg laying feathered critters we all used to have in our back yards. They were our friends who provided us with wholesome food.

But they haven't always been chickens. The English called them fowls (or poultry) and we called them chooks. However, since the invasion of the American mass slaughter houses, those rakeaway money machines that scorched the earth of local, mum and dad shops – like the Colonel's Fricken Tired Chicken and so on – we now all call them chickens. The ones we know today aren't feathered and clucky but very dead, very fatty and served up limply with fat-singed potato strips and cans of toxic lolly water.

Before the American invasion, however, they were live, pecking friends called chooks. Their little, yellow, fluffy babies were called chickens and they grew into pullets and then into chooks.

We normally had around twenty of these busy little madams, constantly digging for worms in our back lawn and they provided eggs for our family and eight shepherds each day. Then, when the time came, we'd choose maybe five, chop their heads off, pluck them in hot water and cook them for Christmas.

They roamed the back lawn like large, rolling snow-flakes, by day, and were herded into the chook run at night – partly to protect them from stoats but mainly to encourage them to sit in the hay-lined boxes to manufacture and plop out our breakfast. The chook run was an area the size of a modern apartment, encircled by six-foot high wire netting. This was abutted against a wooden house that provided protection from the weather, roosting perches and the nesting boxes with little doors through which we gratefully collected their eggy offerings each day.

The chooks were my mother's favourite pets amongst all the others – cats, dogs, pigs, deer, sheep, possums and magpies. They were her little beauties, as she called them, and, thirty years after leaving the farm she can still become weepy as she talks about them.

But she wasn't always popular with them.

She had no interest in trying out the new Suzuki 50 farm bikes when they arrived but us blokes loved a burn-up and just knew she'd love it when she got on. It took a week of persuasion and she finally agreed to learn to ride one of these new fangled machines … probably more to shut us up than from any interest on her part.

Dad kick-started it for her and she leapt back in fright, her hands to her mouth as she quickly backed away. We herded her back as we would a frightened child and she was soon astride the dangerously puttering machine.

Us three boys and Dad gave her enthusiastically simultaneous instructions and she now looked confused as well as frightened. Dad told us to shut up while he gave her the step-by-step of motorcycle motivation.

Her left hand gingerly pulled in the clutch, her left foot clicked into first gear and she smiled wanly as nothing happened. We gave her a moment to relax into that moment of stillness but her left hand flagged and the bike leapt into action. As it shot forward, her right hand gripped the accelerator and it shot forward faster and faster … across the lawn, under the clothes line, through a flock of squawking chooks, between startled dogs, into and out of the ditch with her bum off the seat, her screams ringing out up the gulleys for miles and her right hand pulling the throttle back further and further. What saved her from flying off the edge of the cliff we used as a rubbish tip was the chook run.

She ploughed screaming into the fence and the bike quickly stopped as she created a beautiful wire netting sculpture titled Frantic Woman on Runaway Bike.

It took some time for us to stop rolling in the dirt, laughing our heads off, but we eventually composed ourselves, looked suitably grave while suppressing giggles, and it took a good ten minutes to untangle her from her amazing netting sculpture and a day to mend the chook run.

Mum never went near a motorbike again.

For days she apologised to the chooks. I'm not sure if they gave her the forgiveness she craved but they sure produced a whole lot of eggs the following week!

Chooks were a big part of my life and my language and, somewhere around four years old, I saw my first airborne machine – a topdressing plane that swooped up the gulleys and over the hills, farting its magnificent powder behind it.

For a moment I was transfixed by this terrifyingly bizarre apparition and then, apparently, rushed to Mum, grabbed her apron, pointed skywards and yelled, "Look Mum, a chookie car-car, a chookie car-car!"

From that day to this I have striven to express myself in language equally descriptive and eloquent.

The Old Woman Who Lived In A Shoe

Carole Aveley

There was an old woman who lived in a shoe. She had so many children she didn't know what to do. She gave them some broth, without any bread, whipped them all soundly and sent them to bed.

Well, what do you think they did then? They climbed up the boot laces onto the roof and one by one they scrambled over the tiles into the overhanging branches of their ancient fir tree. The older ones helped the little ones climb down to the ground and away they went! Over the style, through the field and out of sight.

The first house they spied was in darkness, they tip-toed in and found a huge pot of porridge on the wood burning stove. There were three bowls on the kitchen table, with three spoons beside them. Each child dipped a spoon into the porridge for a taste – it was very good. They dipped again and again until they had eaten it all up! It was very cosy in the kitchen beside the stove, glowing with logs in the grate, so they settled themselves on the comfy sofa and fell asleep. In the morning Mama Bear came downstairs and found ten little bodies squeezed together on her sofa, and an empty porridge pot on the table!!

"Be off with you!" she growled, chasing them outside, brandishing her enormous wooden spoon. So off they scurried into the woods in a big hurry.

After wandering most of the day they were quite lost, but they discovered an enticing little cottage tucked away under the trees. It was made of gingerbread with sugar plumbs, liquorice allsorts and smarties stuck all over it. The children were ravenous by then, so they helped themselves to some chocolate icing on the window ledges, and finding it quite delicious, they broke off pieces of marzipan to nibble.

A loud voice demanded, "Who gave you permission to help yourselves to my tasty treats?" A menacing figure dressed in a long black cloak and a tall pointed hat, appeared in the doorway. She grabbed the eldest boy, pinching his cheeks and pulling his ears, making him squeal! And she tried to drag him inside, but the other children charged at her all together, bowling her over and running off before she could regain her feet.

They ran and ran in fright until they were exhausted and then collapsed under a huge old oak tree.

"What are we going to do?" wailed the littlest child. "Nobody wants us!" After a while they noticed a wooden door in the base of the tree, so they knocked. A face peeped out. It was a tiny pixie with pointed ears, who smiled kindly at them. After they told him their sad story he suggested that they climb up the tree into the lower branches where they would find lots of nuts to eat. What luck! As they were munching nuts a squirrel peered at them from his window.

"If you climb higher you will find cherries," he said crossly. "Leave my nuts alone!" So they climbed to the next level and eagerly tucked into the glossy red cherries. A wise old owl sat watching them from his veranda.

"What kind of tree is this?" they asked, "with nuts and cherries and maybe even more goodies higher up?"

"This is the magic Far Away Tree," he replied. "If you climb right to the top where the tree meets the clouds, you will find that you can step out into the clouds and they will carry you far away."

So that is what they did and they found a whole new country where there were no mean old step mothers to beat them, no bears to chase them and no wicked witches threatening to kidnap them.

And they lived happily ever after!

Drinking Beer

Paul Howlett

Drinking beer on a hot summers day
For better or worse you may say
It quenches the thirst of many a man
Who often could not give a damn
For the questions of folk and their ilk
Who want us all to drink milk
Their small little minds cannot be kind
To the joys of drinking lager, beer n wine
To them it is all wicked booze
But to connoisseurs and drinker alike
They will always stay n win the fight.

Abbey Road Party

Paul Howlett

The phone rang at the desk in my office one day in the early 1990s. It was a call from my old friend Charlie.

"Guess what," said Charlie, his voice full of excitement. "You won't believe this," he continued without letting me answer. "I won a trip to England!"

"How did you do that?" I enquired rather mystified.

"I bought two bottles of beer and entered the receipt for them into the promotion box in the drive – in bottle shop!"

"Wow," I exclaimed, "Let me carry your bags!" I jokingly said at the end of the conversation.

Three days later it was no joke as Charlie rang me up and said that I was to accompany him on a ten day trip to England on a Beatles "Rock and Roll" Discovery Tour .

As my friend was giving me a free ride to England, I said that I would provide the spending money.

A month later we had to cross the USA on our way to England and we forgot to check visa requirements for the USA.

On arrival at the airport we were told that we had to have visas for the USA. I did not think that we needed them as we were only travelling across the USA without a stop. I forgot that when you land in the USA, anywhere in the USA, you have to clear customs for a transfer to your next plane. I was used to Asian airports, where you did not have to leave the customs free zone inside the airport. The USA does not work in the same way.

We had some trouble with our transfers at LAX in Los Angeles as they wanted to lock us up in a room at the airport, even as they had our passports and tickets. We disputed the fact of being locked up in a room and spent the time in a bar close to the lock-up! We reported back when our next flight was due to leave and thankfully boarded a plane for England. If it happened today we would not have been allowed to travel across the USA at all!!

More embarrassing moments were to happen on this trip.

We arrived in Manchester airport, England, and we were transported to a nice hotel in Liverpool for a three day tour of Beatle sites and other touristy exhibitions. We took the Magical Mystery Tour bus and drank beer in The Cavern, the downstairs venue where The Beatles commenced their rise to worldwide fame.

After three days in Liverpool we took a train to London, and we were housed in a shiny white expensive hotel.

Our tour bus driver for London was an Aussie who owned the bus that transported us all over London for several days.

The highlight of the London stay was a party at Abbey Road Studios with free food and lots of booze.

In the morning, my friend Charlie wanted to go to Harrods and do some shopping, which would have bored me to death, so I said that I had a plan to do some touristy visits and left Charlie to go shopping.

I caught the tube to Hampton Court, spent a couple of delightful hours checking out the place, bought some souvenirs and caught the tube back to the London hotel with only half an hour to spare.

Catching the tube back to the hotel required several changes in the underground tube system, but I was back at the hotel and in my room with about twenty minutes to shower and change. I need to put on some respectable clothes for the party.

I dived into the shower, quickly soaped and rinsed off. Dried myself and stepped out stark naked into the room to dress myself.

Just as I stepped out of the bathroom, the door to the hotel room suddenly opened and a lady walked to the room.

I looked at her, and she looked at my naked body and said that she was the senior chamber maid for the hotel and was checking out that the room was properly maintained.

I am sure that she was also checking me out. I was rather embarrassed to say the least. She left and I, red-faced, struggled to get all my clothes on in time to catch the bus for the tour of Abbey Road studios.

Charlie, meanwhile, had prepared himself some time before and was reading the local newspaper when I walked out into the hotel foyer.

I told him of my adventures, the trip to and from Hampton Court Palace and my embarrassing encounter with the senior chamber maid.

Charlie asked who was the most embarrassed. I replied that it was probably me, as I am sure most hotel chamber maids see plenty of naked bodies in their course of work!

I was really embarrassed, I reiterated to Charlie as we boarded the bus.

The party at Abbey Road Studios was great.

The Missing Links

Philip J Bradbury

*L*inks is the old Scottish word for that thin strip of wasteland between the sea and the pasture, where sailors would find pieces of wood to hit stones around with. The wild Scots were happy with the impromptu nature of their game but the English, tidy little prats that they were, decided to tidy up Scotland, a messy country. They slaughtered and disowned tens of thousands of carefree lads and lassies from their beloved glens and uplands and gave this wild and untidy landscape to tidy English lords and ladies.

In the process, they tidied up the game of Links by moving it from wasteland to productive farmland, slaughtering and disowning thousands of wild and carefree cows and sheep. They also insisted that it was for men only … perhaps women were too untidy. And so a new name was created for this wonderfully tidy activity – golf, standing for Gentlemen Only, Ladies Forbidden.

Though women are now allowed to join in the swinging, the content of the game has changed little in the last 150 years. However, the form has changed considerably from rich gits in funny clothes … actually, no, it hasn't changed a bit!

So, how is it played?

First, we have a ball. No, not a big soft thing like a football but one with inverted acne that's small enough to become easily lost in the long grass … actually, any grass at all! – and hard enough that it will maim you should it pass nearby.

Secondly, we have to move this elusive little killer around. No, we don't kick it or throw it – that would be too easy. Golfers insist on hitting the ball with a club but it's not one. You see, instead of a hunky lump of wood, which would make it reasonably easy, if you could find your sneaky wee sucker in the long grass. Hey, why make it easy? Instead, they've chosen to build these long, slender lengths of pipe with a knob on the end.

With your knob-ended stick, you have to whack your tarty ball, innocently resting in the long grass or wherever you last belted it to, into a tiny hole in the ground. They make this easy by mowing large runways of grass to a millimetre of its life so you can always find your ball.

However, since the aim of the game is to hit tiny acne into this tiny hole with less thwacks that everyone else, they also add challenges. So, along these grass runways they plant hundreds of trees and dig acres of lakes and sandpits to make it tricky. They usually add a bend or two just so you can never tell where that stupid hole in the ground is till you trip in it and break your ankle.

The idea of the game was to get much needed exercise but now they've added wheels to your bag of clubs and then invented push-chairs so you don't have to walk anywhere. Some places even issue balls with GPS systems in them so you can easily find your balls. Make the balls hard to find and then add GPS so they're easy to find … yes, it was rich gits who created this bizarre game so we shouldn't expect any logic, should we?

The professionals even have other people to pull their wheeled bags around, saving them even more exercise. These bag-pullers are called caddies and it can be a well-paid job. In 2012, New Zealand's highest paid sportsman was Tiger Woods' caddie. Did I mention wealthy gits wearing funny clothes?

So, let's start playing. You belt this little dimply ball half a mile into a hole you can't see as it's on the other side of a twenty-acre forest and the easy bits of the land are festooned with pesky ponds and mini deserts. It's also interrupted by other golfers, going the other way, who could get a bonk on the conk if either of you are less than attentive. You must do this eighteen times. Yes, there's eighteen little holes dotted over the vast crumpled estate and the person who whacks his ball the least number of times is the winner. Golfers tend to roam in packs of four so you just find three chums to compete against, go whack, whack,

whack for a few hours of a weekend and then you've got something to talk about – endlessly and boringly – for the rest of the week.

Aside from handicapped snail racing, golf is the slowest sport on the planet but, despite that, millions of lesser-paid spectators love to watch rich gits getting wealthier by smashing little balls around with knobby pipes. After all, there has to be some compensations for not having a life.

And that is why, my friends, the name of the game – GOLF – has changed from Gentlemen Only, Ladies Forbidden to Gits Owning Limitless Funds.

Limericks

Joan Alexander
There is now a president called Trump,
Who gave his opponents the hump.
When they called him a cheat,
He replied with a tweet,
You can all take a long running jump.

Estelle McCrohan
There was an old man up the creek
Who had really incredible cheek.
He sat in the water
Which he never did oughta –
Fed the freshwater fish for a week!

Judy de la Mare
There once was a poet called Walter ,
Words flowed from his pen without falter,
He wrote with great speed,
Paying spelling no heed,
Yet few words he needed to alter.

Paul Howlett
The was a young man from Bourke
Thought stealing was a good lurk
He bought a big gun
For a trifling sum
And found that it did not work

Mark Grieveson
Malcolm - a climate change denier
Perfectly cast for savage satire
Knows not fact from fiction
And has very poor diction
But he's sure an accomplished liar

Carole Aveley
There was a young lady named Carole
Who got swept over Vic Falls in a barrel
Landing with a thud
Her head in the mud
She dug herself out with a trowel.

Philip J Bradbury
He once had a yearning to write
But his friends said his scribbles were trite
He left in a rush
Turned his brain to mush
And now stands on parliament, on the right

NK
A monkey and goose were to wed
Both wearing some pink and some red
But the monkey got goosebumps
And the goose caught the monkey lumps
And they ended up really quite dead

Janet Findlay
There was an old woman from Brassall
Who decided that clothes were a hassle
So when it was hot
She wore not a jot
And when it was cold - a tassle!

Biographies

Carole Aveley

Born in Yorkshire. I attended nine schools and lived in six countries. I became a bookkeeper, then ran my own gardening business. After being widowed twice, Australia beckoned and life is now full of irresistible opportunities!

Estelle McCrohan

I have had an extremely varied life. Travel throughout Australia on land and sea gave me the opportunity to write articles for lifestyle magazines which became a book. I enjoy helping people write about their lives and run writing workshops. Different experiences have culminated in fiction and non-fiction works and I continue writing with varying degrees of enthusiasm! You can find me at https://joycemcc.wordpress.com/ and my books are available at Lulu.com.

Books that I have written include Red Earth, Blue Seas (Australian adventures), Dance of Deception (romantic novel), Pebbles Along the Way (inspirational book) and Capture Your Life in Writing (guide to writing your autobiography or memoir).

Janet Findley

Janet has been an actor, performance poet and radio copywriter. She has co-written several shows - one of which was performed at the Edinburgh Fringe Festival. Most recently, she has been one half of the music/comedy duo The Babbling Trillbillys and occasionally, reprises her impersonation of the Queen.

Jenny Chriswick

Jenny hails from England where she was educated and commenced her working career on major construction projects. In her mid-twenties she went to work in NZ and the south pacific islands and, later, Australia and international projects. This exposed her to many different cultures and interesting people. After years of writing factual reports she finds that creative writing is very liberating and most enjoyable.

NK

I was born
I will die
I have lived
I have loved
I have cried
And I've laughed.
What else would you like to know?

A bio's a boast
It reads like a toast
To an author who's written a page.
But it's written by me
And surely you see
That instead of the "I"
I am forced to write 'she'.

As though it was written by
Some other person
In praise of the person
That's actually me.

We all know that I wrote it
And no one will quote it
So I'll keep my secrets
You see.

But I hope that you'll read me
And enjoy my quite quirky
Stories written so Eloquently.

Joan Alexander

Joan was born in Shanghai. After Pearl Harbour, her father was interned. Joan, with her mother and brother, were sent to England in exchange for Japanese nationals. The Family was reunited post war in Australia. Joan was educated in Sydney and Katoomba. Life-long friends were made during nursing training at Royal Prince Alfred Hospital, Sydney. She is Married with three children, settled in Queensland and worked at Ipswich Hospital and Domiciliary nursing.

Although never having done any creative writing before, has thoroughly enjoyed the summer school and loves U3A.

Judy de la Mare

Judy worked for over forty years as a medical scientist but has always had a passion for the arts. She enjoys creating interesting things from nature – sculptures from clay, textiles from wool, gardens from the earth. She also loves reading and writing.

Mark Grieveson

1950's vintage autodidact and connoisseur of the road less travelled.

Paul Howlett

Writing is a passion of mine for many years. I am learning foreign languages I like reading, scuba diving and travel.

Philip J Bradbury

I was born very early in life and started writing soon after, only to abandon it when the trappings of responsibility – marriage, jobs, children, looking good – flounced at my feet. Having now outgrown any responsibility garnered to date, I have become an irresponsible old man, have written 18 books to date, run writing groups, run a training company, cycle and yoga a lot and my alter-ego can be found on the internet at www.philipjbradbury.com

Appendix

Page 10 answer: Making a lamp, which Carole's husband did as a business.

Page 25 answer: Fitting tiller and rudder assembly to yacht while afloat, something Estelle's partner became adept at in moments of forgetfulness.

Page 42 answer: Throwing a pot, as in pottery, not cooking!